Perfect Redundancy
and how to survive it

THE PERFECT SERIES

OTHER TITLES IN THE SERIES:

The Perfect Appraisal by Howard Hudson
Perfect Assertiveness by Jan Ferguson
The Perfect Business Plan by Ron Johnson
Perfect Business Writing by Peter Bartram
The Perfect Career by Max Eggert
Perfect Communications by Andrew Leigh and Michael Maynard
The Perfect Conference by Iain Maitland
The Perfect Consultant by Max Eggert and Elaine van der Zeil
Perfect Counselling by Max Eggert
Perfect Customer Care by Ted Johns
The Perfect CV by Max Eggert
Perfect Decisions by Andrew Leigh
The Perfect Dismissal by John McManus
Perfect Empowerment by Sarah Cook and Steve Macaulay
Perfect Executive Health by Dr Andrew Melhuish
Perfect Financial Ratios by Terry Gasking
Perfect Freelancing by Sean Marriott and Paula Jacobs
Perfect In-house Training by Colin Jones-Evans
The Perfect Interview by Max Eggert
The Perfect Leader by Andrew Leigh and Michael Maynard
Perfect Marketing by Louella Miles
The Perfect Meeting by David Sharman
The Perfect Negotiation by Gavin Kennedy
Perfect PR by Marie Jennings
Perfect Pensions by Barbara Ellis
Perfect People Skills by Andrew Floyer Acland
Perfect Personal Finance by Marie Jennings
Perfect Presentation by Andrew Leigh and Michael Maynard
Perfect Quality by Bryn Owen
Perfect Recruitment by David Oates and Viv Shackleton
Perfect Relaxation by Elaine van der Zeil
The Perfect Report by Peter Bartram
The Perfect Sale by Nick Thornely and Dan Lees
Perfect Stress Control by Carole McKenzie
Perfect Teamwork by Ron Johnson
Perfect Time Management by Ted Johns

Perfect Redundancy
and how to survive it

**ALL YOU NEED
TO GET IT RIGHT
FIRST TIME**

LYNN WILLIAMS

ARROW
BUSINESS BOOKS

Published by Arrow Books in 1997

1 3 5 7 9 10 8 6 4 2

© Lynn Williams 1997

Lynn Williams has asserted her rights under the Copyright, Designs and Patents Act, 1988 to be identified as the author of this work.

This book is sold subject to the condition that it shall not, by way of trade or otherwise, be lent, resold, hired out, or otherwise circulated without the publisher's prior consent in any form of binding or cover other than that in which it is published and without a similar condition including this condition being imposed on the subsequent purchaser.

First published by
Arrow Books Limited
20 Vauxhall Bridge Road, London SW1V 2SA

Random House Australia (Pty) Limited
20 Alfred Street, Milsons Point
Sydney, New South Wales 2061, Australia

Random House New Zealand Limited
18 Poland Road, Glenfield
Auckland 10, New Zealand

Random House South Africa (Pty) Limited
Endulini, 5a Jubilee Road, Parktown 2193, South Africa

Papers used by Random House UK Limited are natural, recyclable products made from wood grown in sustainable forests. The manufacturing processes conform to the environmental regulations of the country of origin.

Companies, institutions and other organizations wishing to make bulk purchases of any business books published by Random House should contact their local bookstore or Random House direct:
Special Sales Director
Random House
20 Vauxhall Bridge Road
London SW1V 2SA
Tel: 0171 840 8470 Fax: 0171 828 6681

Random House UK Limited Reg. No. 954009
ISBN 0 09 922432 1

Set in Bembo by
SX Composing DTP, Rayleigh, Essex
Printed and bound in Great Britain by
Cox & Wyman Ltd., Reading, Berkshire

British Cataloguing in Publication Data
A catalogue record for this book is available from the British Library

CONTENTS

Introduction 1

Redundancy: What happens? 3

Part One: THINGS THAT HELP

1. **Structure** 11

2. **Confidence** 23

3. **Security** 34

4. **Goals** 49

Part Two: THINGS THAT MAY GET IN THE WAY

5. **Stress** 63

6. **Worry** 71

7. **Anger** 79

8. **Apathy** 86

9. **Depression** 92

Conclusion: Ten positive steps 103

INTRODUCTION

This is a somewhat different book to the one that I initially planned. Originally, I had intended to look at the different stages that we go through as we come to terms with redundancy, and to look at the process of coming to terms with change.

Much of what I had previously wanted to say is still included here. However, while I was researching the information about redundancy and unemployment that I needed, I read many studies and reports about how different people coped with it in different ways.

Some people handled job loss very badly, becoming depressed and demoralized and, ultimately, fatalistic about it. Others, though in very similar circumstances, seemed to be much more resilient and survived better.

A lot of the reports were, understandably, about groups who had failed to cope effectively with unemployment – who had ended up defeated by their circumstances and without hope.

It didn't seem to make any difference whether these were short or long terms of unemployment. Some long-term unemployed people remained realistically optimistic about their futures and were working steadily towards personal goals. In contrast, some people who had been unemployed for only a relatively short period had already given up on their personal objectives and showed signs of psychological debility.

Reading these, what I became interested in was looking at the groups, and people within groups, who had coped *well* with unemployment. I wanted to know:

- What had they done that increased their chances of survival?
- How, exactly, had they done it?
- Was it some action that they took for themselves?
- Was it just chance circumstances that helped them?
- Did they have anything in common?
- Was there anything special that they did that non-copers didn't do?
- Was it due to intrinsic factors such as age, class, or gender?

In the end, it seemed clear that people who survive redundancy have several things in common. While there is no one, big secret, they do tend to do certain things and hold certain attitudes. And when things get them down, they look after themselves in particular ways.

This book looks at what these mechanisms are, and attempts to give advice on how you can recreate these conditions, using tried and tested techniques. You, too, can survive . . .

REDUNDANCY: WHAT HAPPENS?

For many of us, losing our job is the most traumatic event we will ever go through, except for losing a loved one.

However sensitively it has been handled, we will probably, at some time, experience feelings of anger, dismay, rejection, self-doubt, and disbelief. In fact, there is often a distinct pattern to the feelings associated with job loss – several stages which work themselves out over a period of time.

We each go through these stages in our own way, at our own pace. For some, they occur in an orderly sequence; for others, they repeat in cycles over a period of time. For everyone, some things will be easier to cope with than others.

We need time to settle down again and adjust to the new shape of our lives after the crisis. The pattern of feelings is like the series of aftershocks that follow an earthquake. They may be severe at first, but they gradually ease with time.

The patterns of adjustment after redundancy can be divided into three main stages:

1. **The initial response**
2. **The intermediate phase**
3. **Settling down.**

1. The Initial Response
The feelings typical of this stage are:

- Numbness
- Denial

- Confusion
- Unreal optimism

When the news is first broken, the shock can be a bit too much to take on board immediately. You cannot quite believe that it's happened. There is a feeling of numbness and unreality.

Gradually, the truth sinks in but it may bring with it feelings of confusion.

It is not unusual for people to wonder if there hasn't been some sort of mistake, or if it's all a practical joke. Some may find themselves obsessionally going over the past few weeks or months, wondering what they could have done differently.

For some time afterwards, you may feel that this is just a temporary stage, and that you will soon find another job, if not this week, then next.

You may take this as an opportunity to have a break, and people sometimes spend large amounts of their redundancy settlement on the holiday of a lifetime. You may also feel that, as this is only a temporary set-back, there is no point in signing on and claiming benefit.

2. The Intermediate Phase
The feelings typical of this stage are:

- Worry
- Panic
- Anger
- Grief
- Unreal pessimism

After the initial response, negative feelings may start to surface. Disbelief may be replaced by anger, unreal optimism by worry, numbness by grief. You may begin to fantasize about getting your own back, or imagine yourself and your family ending up begging in the street.

Even thinking about money may cause feelings of panic. Rather than taking practical steps towards claiming benefits due to you and assessing your resources for the future, you may find yourself despairing or getting angry at the very mention of planning or budgeting.

Just as there may have been a lack of emotion in the previous stage, there may be an excess of emotion in this, as if it has all been saved up for now.

The first few job applications fail. You may feel bitter and rejected and begin to wonder if you are still employable. You may find yourself wondering if you would be fit for work even it if were offered.

It is at this stage that boredom and isolation can begin to set in. As your self-esteem diminishes, you may find yourself avoiding friends and acquaintances, not knowing how to tell them that you are unemployed.

You may begin to think of yourself as 'unemployed', as if it is a job title. You may, consequently, find it hard to know what to say when people ask you what you do – another source of social isolation.

3. Settling Down
The feelings typical of this stage are:

- Acceptance or resignation
- Realistic optimism or hopelessness
- Purposefulness or defeat

The final stage is the one that you will probably settle down to at last. It is the stage in which you finally adjust to becoming unemployed. There are, however, two distinctly different ways of doing this. Acceptance of the situation can be:

- *Resigned acceptance*
- *Constructive acceptance*

Resigned acceptance

This is a negative continuation of the previous stage – you become resigned to unemployment. Boredom and isolation, bitterness and rejection increase, and a long downward spiral commences. You identify yourself as one of 'the unemployed', and you become increasingly deskilled. Your aspirations reduce, and you may become more and more withdrawn. There is a real possibility of depression.

Your search for work becomes increasingly sporadic and is pursued with little sense of hope or expectation.

Constructive acceptance

You come to terms with your anger and grief, accept the reality of unemployment, and make realistic plans for the future. You are able to look at the situation clearly and adapt accordingly. You are able to tolerate your circumstances, but you hope for better and take active, practical steps to achieve it.

Your search for work is focused and energetic, but not obsessional. You may make this an opportunity to take stock of your working life to date and consider your future direction.

Whether you settle down to *resigned* or *constructive* acceptance depends less on chance than on specific coping strategies. The people who survive redundancy, who reach a state of constructive acceptance and maintain their readiness for future work, are found to have ways of dealing with unemployment that help them to retain their positive outlook.

There are a number of things you can do that, taken together, significantly increase your chances of ensuring that you reach a constructive outcome:

- Replace the structures of 'real work' with new ones
- Build up your confidence and self-esteem
- Rebuild your security
- Plan for your future

In this book, we shall look at how you can actually carry out these four activities. It is divided into two parts:

- Part One: Things That Help

This part looks at the things that will help you to survive redundancy and achieve a constructive outcome.

- Part Two: Things That May Get in the Way

This part takes a closer look at those negative feelings that may prevent you from coming through successfully, and talks about how you can overcome them.

Part One:
THINGS THAT HELP

This section looks at the positive things that you can do to help yourself achieve a constructive recovery from redundancy.

These can be summed up as:

- **Rebuilding structures**

- **Rebuilding confidences**

- **Rebuilding security**

- **Setting goals**

Each chapter first describes what each of these means, suggests why it might help, and then goes on to look at ways that you might put it into practice.

1
STRUCTURE

WHAT IS STRUCTURE?
Work provides a structure for our lives, a framework on which we can shape the timetable for our day, a chance to meet people outside the home, a meaning and purpose for our daily existence.

Work provides a number of different structures:

- **Routine** – we know where we are supposed to be and what we are supposed to be doing. There is time spent at work and time at home; time for business and time for play; time with people and time alone; time to concentrate and time to relax. We plan daily events such as getting up, having meals, leaving the house and coming home, weekends and holidays, around the framework provided by work.
- **Social structure** – work largely dictates whom we see, and when, where, and why we see them. We will see more of some people than others, more of some *types* of people than others. The sort of work that we do and the basis on which we meet these people will largely determine how they will respond to us and treat us. A large part of our identity – the way that others see us and how we see ourselves – will be influenced by the work that we do.
- **Targets** – work imposes many of the goals and targets in our lives. What we aim for is often associated with work. This can be either directly – the attainment levels and objectives of the job – or more indirectly related to the salary or status that we hope to achieve.
- **Purpose** – work provides routines with *meaning*; there is a reason for doing things, even just getting up in the morning.

Such structures gives us a balance to our lives – we know what is work and what is leisure so that we know when to switch off and when to stop working. In a good working environment, we also know what is expected of us and have clear targets so that we know when we have reached them.

Often, we are more confident dealing with people in our working role – where we know what they expect of us and how to handle the problems.

The balance between work and leisure also gives us some idea of when it is appropriate to be formal, and when we can relax and enjoy ourselves.

For many people, it is work that gives the motivation to look after themselves. They ensure that they get enough sleep to be fresh for work in the morning. They eat well so that they have the energy they need for work. They take care of their grooming and personal appearance because they need to do so for work. They ensure that they take sufficient time off and get enough relaxation so that they can cope effectively with work.

WHY DOES REBUILDING STRUCTURE HELP?

When you lose your job, the structure of your everyday life becomes vulnerable. It is fatally easy, over a period of weeks or months, to find that days slide into a rut of monotony.

Without work to provide routine, days can become chaotic and meaningless. Isolation begins to set in as social contact becomes reduced. Motivation flags as aims and objectives are lost sight of. The less you do, the less you *feel* like doing, and the less you feel *able* to do.

Studies of people who have become unemployed show that those who replace the framework that work provides with structures of their own, achieve several benefits:

- They stay 'job ready' and feel competent to take on new work roles.
- They avoid isolation by retaining social contacts.
- They retain a greater degree of optimism.
- They sustain their psychological resilience – coping with the ups and downs better.
- They maintain their physical health.
- Their job search remains active and focused.
- They avoid many of the negative effects of job loss such as excessive stress, depression, low self-esteem, negative self-image, or destructive behaviour (excessive drinking, smoking, and so on).
- They retain their senses of identity, worth, and motivation.

The best structures are those that supply the things that come from paid employment – routine, social contact, aims and objectives. But it's also helpful to acknowledge the greater flexibility now possible. Good structures and timetables allow for new experiences that may formerly have been impossible or overlooked in the everyday rush and bustle of work.

Now that there is time, new hobbies or neglected interests and pursuits can be timetabled into the schedule as a worthwhile part of the day. Attention to health and well-being can be part of the new structure. Education can be continued and involvement in voluntary projects is now an option. Adult education classes and leisure facilities are often available at concessionary rates to those registered as unemployed. Travel, or use of public facilities, may be cheaper at off-peak periods.

The people that survive redundancy best, and look back on it with a positive attitude, build their own new frameworks.

REBUILDING STRUCTURE: WHAT TO DO

One of the main keys to surviving redundancy and unemployment is to actively build new structures in your life to replace the ones you lost along with your job.

If you can start planning this before you leave work, so much the better. Catch up on all the things you always meant to do, but set a time limit. When this ends, put your new plans into effect – do not slide into lethargy and non-employment.

You need to:

- Timetable your day
- Maintain your social contacts
- Set yourself targets
- Develop your personal sense of purpose

Timetable your day

Decide what your days should include. Remember to include both the things you *need* to do and the things you *want* to do. Take the opportunity to incorporate activities that you couldn't do when you were at work.

Things that you may want to think about could be:

- **Spending time with your family** – many people at work would like more time for family and friends. The chance to become more involved with their children's daily activities is something that many who have been through redundancy look back on very positively.
- **Updating and upgrading skills and education** – catch up on developments in your area now that you have the time. Read magazines and new publications – your local library should be able to help. Take advantage of any concessionary rates on courses or adult education classes to expand existing skills – improve

keyboard skills, gain a formal qualification in computer literacy, learn a second language, etc.

If a lack of formal qualifications or specific skills is holding you back, now is the time to do something about it.

- **Pursuing interests** – spend time acquiring or developing the skills you didn't have time for when you were at work all day. Get more involved with any clubs or organizations that you belong to.
- **Job hunting** – this has to be a major consideration. Plan your time to include:
  - Researching job opportunities
  - Networking
  - Writing speculative letters
  - Writing applications
  - Attending interviews
  - Reading newspapers, magazines, bulletins, etc. for advertised vacancies
  - Making speculative calls
  - Reviewing and updating skills and experience
- **Exercise** – physical activity will ease tensions and frustration and improve your physical fitness.
- **Relaxation** – it can sometimes be tempting to think that as you are not 'really working' you don't deserve to relax. Being unemployed – coping with redundancy, looking for another job – can be quite stressful, however, and you do need to take time off.
- **Socialising** – as well as family and close friends, make time to be with others both employed and unemployed. Employed friends and acquaintances will be able to help you network and pass on job leads, gossip, and information. Unemployed friends and acquaintances will provide support, understanding, and fellow feeling.

Aim for balance – It's tempting to feel the need to spend twenty-four hours a day looking for another job. Include balance and variety in your day otherwise you may become stale and unproductive, and not get the most out of this period of your life.

Plan a good mixture of things every day. Balance and moderation will help to keep a sense of proportion and reduce stress.

Create boundaries – In a well-planned working day, you know when it's time to start and stop. Aim for the same sense of balance in your new timetable and set definite boundaries between activities.

Mealtimes are useful for doing this, but other boundaries could be:

- tea or coffee breaks
- taking a walk
- bathing, showering or changing clothes
- changing location – moving from the room where you always write your application letters to the room where you always watch television, for example.

Unless you have urgent tasks to perform, stick to these boundaries, divide the day up to ensure a balance of work, rest, and play. Without clear boundaries, morning slips into afternoon and afternoon into evening. Tasks are either left 'until tomorrow' or spill over into rest and leisure times, creating a sense of boredom and staleness.

Plan for flexibility – Interviews may come up at any time, and you need to be sure that you can attend. Use the freedom you now have to plan ahead and take advantage of cheap rates or concessions.

Please yourself – You can do what you like, when you like, so use your time effectively. If you are best in the mornings, do the difficult or demanding things then. Save the afternoons for the more routine tasks. Try not to drift too far from normal working hours – going back to work or even getting up on time for interviews will not be such a shock to the system.

Example

Early morning	Visit Computer Centre at College of Further Education. Continue AmiPro tutorial. Check information board.
Mid morning	Break. Have coffee and chat to tutors.
Late morning	Library. See if any interesting new periodicals are in – copy likely job vacancies. Check local directories for appropriate companies, take details for speculative calls or letters. Check directories for information about the company interviewing me next week.
Lunch	Prepare lunch. Go for walk. Buy newspaper.
Early afternoon	Ring job advertisements for application forms. Ring company offering interview, ask for annual report and in-house journal. Ring two contact names on list for information. Follow up two speculative letters from last week with a phone call.
Mid afternoon	Break. Have tea and start new novel picked up at library.
Late afternoon	Your turn to collect children from school. Go to park on way home. Spend time on activity with them at home.
Evening meal	Eat and relax.
Early evening	Prepare two speculative letters.
Mid evening	Break. Have coffee. Chat to partner about their day.
Late evening	Relax watching television.

This timetable includes a balance of work, rest and play and takes advantage of a flexible schedule to spend time with family.

There are plenty of job search activities planned, but they

are nicely varied and interspersed with other things.

Each day would have a different schedule – the next day, for example, might include an early afternoon swim to take advantage of cheap rates, and an adult education class in the early evening.

MAINTAIN YOUR SOCIAL CONTACTS

Unemployment can be a very isolating experience unless you plan for it.

Take steps to make sure that you have social contact even though you are not going out to work every day, and may have financial restraints. You need support and encouragement from other people, as well as the chance to forget about problems in good company.

The people who survive redundancy best, replace the timetable that work imposed with a flexible timetable of their own. Similarly, those who avoid isolation and loneliness do so by replacing the social structure that work provides with a framework of their own.

Some of the ways of maintaining social contacts that have worked for others in the past include:

- Forming a social or support group with other colleagues made redundant at the same time.
- Forming or joining a local unemployed workers centre or support network.
- Joining local associations that are nothing to do with unemployment or work:
    - Environmental networks
    - Community groups
    - Special interest groups
    - Sports teams
- Becoming more active in your trade union or professional association.

- Doing voluntary work.
- Joining a job club (eligible after six months unemployment).
- Attending training courses and adult education classes.
- Taking time to compile a 'contact list' of neglected friends and colleagues, and keeping in regular contact with them.
- Helping out in a pub. (For payment in kind – you should not be working and drawing unemployment benefit at the same time.)
- Joining local LETS scheme (Local Employment and Trade System – a bartering network where you exchange skills instead of money).

Stay in touch with your ex-colleagues and work contacts in addition to building up new social structures. They will form the basis of your network when you are looking for information and advice in your job hunt.

SET YOURSELF TARGETS

Setting yourself targets and achieving them helps your confidence and self-esteem. Make your targets realistic, and make sure that they are clear.

Targets need to be simple and precise, otherwise it can be difficult to know when you have achieved them. It is also useful to break large goals down into small targets – getting a job, for example, is a large goal. You are more likely to achieve it if you set smaller targets that will help you to get there, such as:

- Update your CV and bring it up to professional standard.
- List all the companies in your field and contact three each week for information.
- Compile a detailed contact list, and get in touch with four names every week.
- Get up to date and read one specialist journal in your

field every week.

The sort of monthly targets you could set yourself might include:

- Read two books on an unfamiliar topic every month.
- Attend an evening class on a subject that interests you.
- Try doing a familiar thing in a different way.
- Do those maintenance jobs that you always meant to get round to.

Make a note of your targets and congratulate yourself every time you achieve one.

DEVELOP A PERSONAL SENSE OF PURPOSE

Developing a sense of purpose depends a lot on finding out what you think and feel is important to you, and planning what to do about it. This is covered in the section on *goals* on p.49–60.

Being in work provides us with more than just pay. Work, whatever the job, gives rewards that we value in different ways.

In order to maintain a sense of purpose, people who survive redundancy well will often find ways to achieve these rewards from other sources.

Think about what you get from work. Apart from money, some of the things that others have suggested include:

- A feeling of involvement
- Social contact
- A structured day
- Shared experiences
- A sense of status
- The chance to exercise skills and knowledge
- The chance to acquire skills and knowledge

- Making a valued contribution
- A sense of moving forward
- Achievement
- Being of service to others

Think about other sources, as well as work, where you get these rewards at present. Where might you get them from in the future?

Example

Reward	Present Source	Additional Future Source
The chance to acquire skills and knowledge	Interest in art and antiques – reading about and talking to others.	Course on art history. Join appreciation group. Make full use of concessions at museum and art gallery
Shared experiences	Friends. Professional Association.	Job club (after six months).
The chance to exercise skills and knowledge	Volunteer coach in life-skills at rehabilitation centre.	Increase involvement at centre. Pass on technical work skills as volunteer at youth centre.

Frequently used alternative sources and the sort of reward they might give are shown in the table on the following page.

PERFECT REDUNDANCY

Reward	Education or Training	Part-time work	Job club or similar	Voluntary or community work
A feeling of involvement		✓		✓
Social contact	✓	✓	✓	✓
Shared experiences		✓	✓	✓
A sense of status				✓
The chance to exercise skills and knowledge		✓		✓
The chance to acquire skills and knowledge	✓	✓	✓	✓
Making a valued contribution		✓		✓
A sense of moving forward	✓	✓	✓	✓
Achievement	✓	✓		✓
Being of service to others				✓

2
CONFIDENCE

WHAT IS CONFIDENCE?
Confidence is a reasonable belief in yourself and your abilities based on a rational assessment of what you expect to achieve.

Confidence and self-esteem are helpful qualities to have – from them springs the certainty that, whatever happens, you will survive.

People who are confident are able to withstand knocks and setbacks because they basically believe that they are competent and of value to the world. This makes them more resilient than someone who lacks confidence.

They adapt well to new situations because they believe they have succeeded in the past, and can do so again. Criticism and rejection, although they still hurt, do little fundamental damage to their self-esteem. At heart, they know their own worth. They are able to see negative reactions objectively, and even learn from them.

Confident people usually treat other people with respect, too. Because they value themselves, they can see the value in others.

Confidence should not be confused with over-confidence. Confidence is based on a carefully built and tested faith and trust in yourself – over-confidence is based on wishful thinking and, often, ignorance of the true situation.

The events that happen during our lives, especially during childhood, can sometimes damage confidence and self-esteem. Fortunately, though, there are ways to build them up again.

Confident behaviour

assertive	good relationships
respect for others	tries new things
respect for self	takes calculated risks
relaxed and friendly	feels equal to others
open-minded	

Unconfident behaviour

aggressive or passive	closed mind
lack of respect for others	suspicious
lack of respect for self	overcautious
feels inferior or superior	timid or shy

WHY DOES REBUILDING CONFIDENCE HELP?

People who survive redundancy best are those who, consciously or unconsciously, do things to rebuild their confidence in *all* areas of their lives.

For many people their job is a major part of their self-image and, with it, their self-esteem.

It comes as a shock to realize that they can no longer rely on this factor. Even the most confident people can feel lost for a while after termination of their employment.

Losing your job is always a blow to your self-esteem. This is true whatever the circumstances, whether you lose it through restructuring, closure, or dismissal. You can be one of hundreds facing mass redundancy, you can be absolutely certain that it is not your fault, yet it still feels like personal rejection.

You need confidence in yourself to survive a setback like redundancy. You also need a high degree of self-belief to keep going through unemployment. You need a lot of confidence to survive the crisis, and get back into the job market.

Job hunting needs a lot of resilience. You need to put yourself across confidently and with assurance.

You not only have to have confidence in yourself, you also have to persuade others to have confidence in you. And, of course, every time you apply for a job, you risk another rejection.

For people whose self-esteem is low, one or two setbacks – a series of negative replies, a couple of poor interviews – is enough to make them very hesitant about pushing themselves any further. They stop applying for jobs and begin to avoid interviews. The stagnation, and lack of any positive feedback that results from this, reduces their confidence even further. Slowly but surely, they begin to slide into a downward spiral of self-doubt. Gradually they come to see themselves as failures – a totally self-fulfilling prophecy.

Those people who are able to maintain and actively build up their confidence and self-esteem during unemployment are found to:

- Come to terms with loss better.
- Cope better with negative emotions such as anger, worry, sadness, and frustration.
- Maintain social links.
- Maintain better relationships with partners.
- Keep themselves constructively occupied.
- Have better physical health.
- Be more resilient psychologically.
- Consider alternative occupations positively.
- Make constructive use of openings that occur.
- Have realistic expectations.

REBUILDING CONFIDENCE: WHAT TO DO

You need to rebuild your confidence on a broad basis after a blow to your self-esteem like redundancy.

Just as you concentrated on rebuilding the structures you lost with your job, channel your attention to what remains. Think about what you have that you can use to rebuild supports rather than concentrating on the props that have been taken away. Build what you can with the bricks that you have, rather than regretting the bricks that are gone.

There are specific things that you can do that will help you to rebuild your confidence and self-esteem:

Look after yourself
- Treat yourself well and look after your health and well-being at a simple, basic level. You are probably in less of a hurry than when you were at work, so have more time to attend to yourself.
- Aim to go back to work fitter, stronger and healthier than when you left.
- Eat well and healthily, especially now you have the time to shop around and prepare food.
- Spend time on exercise and relaxation. Both will build up your resilience and help you to deal better with stress in the future.
- Continue to go to bed and get up at a reasonable time.
- Keep a sense of pride in yourself and your appearance.

Be nice to yourself
Do things that make you feel good, and avoid things that make you feel bad – unless they have some other very obvious pay-off.

Give yourself small treats and rewards to raise your morale.

Reassess past mistakes
Everybody has occasions in their lives when they could have done better, and redundancy often seems to bring out any self-doubts you may have had about your competence at work.

Blaming yourself only undermines confidence and self-esteem, making it harder to try again. What helps to build self-confidence is accepting that you make mistakes, and trying to learn from them.

Perhaps, for example, you let someone down by not sending them a report on time. Thinking about this objectively, you remember that this came about because there was no one available to type it up for you. There was no one around, however, because it was five o'clock on Friday afternoon.

By looking into it further, you may see that this event is part of a wider pattern where you tend to leave things until the last moment and then run into difficulties.

By recognizing and accepting this about yourself, you are now in a stronger position to do something positive and practical, so there will be fewer similar mistakes in future.

You could, for example, get hold of a large year-planner and make sure that you write in when you need to *start* things in order to get them finished on time.

You could reward yourself, from now on, every time you do something promptly instead of letting it hang around.

Use this time away from the pressure of work to iron out these problems and do even better in future.

Take risks

While it is often tempting to seek comfort, we need some challenges in our lives in order to grow and test our own strength.

Being adventurous is stimulating, it builds confidence. Interestingly, as long as the risks are not life-and-death matters, it seems to make little difference whether the outcome is successful or not. It's actually *taking* the risk that encourages self-esteem.

Try some small risks:

- Chat to a friendly-looking stranger
- Enrol for a class in something you know little about but might enjoy
- Apply for a job for which you're not *quite* qualified
- Ring a company and ask to come in and see them for a short chat about prospects
- Try a book by a 'difficult' author
- Try a type of food you've never eaten before
- Offer your services free of charge to a local charity
- Enter a competition
- Write a short article and send it off to your local paper
- Write a letter to the editor of a national paper

Do things that you enjoy

Confidence grows with doing things that you enjoy. You do not, necessarily, have to be that good at what you do, it's the commitment and enthusiasm that you bring to it that are of benefit. Doing something that you can lose yourself in without being unnecessarily conscious of mistakes or shortcomings is a tremendous boost to self-esteem.

Do something new

Like taking risks, being adventurous and doing something new stimulates confidence. Acquiring competence in an area that you have never tried before enhances belief in yourself and your abilities.

Take the opportunity that you now have to add to your skills. Join an adult education class – learn a new language or master the computer at long last. Follow up subjects in your local library – learn speed-reading or expand your interest in Asian cookery.

Decide your goals

Deciding goals and priorities and acting on them is covered in a later section (see p.49–60). Briefly, when you have well-thought-out plans and objectives that reflect your interests and values, you are more likely to work enthusiastically towards them and feel confident that you will achieve them. You are also far more likely to try new things and take calculated risks in pursuit of them.

Take steps to reach your goals

It has been said that if you want to reach the goal, you have to first kick the ball. Once you have decided your goals, whether in life or in work, you need to take regular steps, however small, towards achieving them.

Doing something every day towards achieving your goals helps you to feel that you are getting somewhere. You can feel confident that you are moving forward, and you can look back at how far you have already come.

Develop performance competence

One way to increase your confidence is to improve the skill with which you do something – your performance competence. It can be something that you already do, or something new that you are trying.

How do you improve your performance?

- **Get on with it** – First of all, you actually have to practise the skill you want to develop. Realistically assess the amount of effort that you will need to put into it to become competent and decide if you have the time, self-discipline and enthusiasm necessary. If you decide to go ahead, do not agonize and put it off until you improve or get into the right mood, *just do it*.
- **It doesn't have to be perfect** – It doesn't matter how badly you perform at the beginning, do at least a little regularly. You can expect to do badly and make

mistakes at the start. Be patient with yourself and accept this 'incompetent' stage – don't let perfectionism stand in your way. It is regular and persistent *doing* rather than *doing well* that is important.
- **Break it down into small stages** – Set yourself smaller targets within the broader task. Break each task down into its component parts and work through each stage in turn. Chart small improvements – if, for example, you want to increase your typing speed up to sixty words a minute, aim first for twenty-five words a minute, then thirty words, and so on. Progress towards your goal of competency in small steps rather than trying to do it in one Olympic-sized jump.
- **Look at the results** – We learn, grow and improve by studying the results of what we do – looking at the feedback. Think about what you did well this time, and what you would do differently next time. You may notice that there are areas that could repay greater concentration in future, or perhaps areas that you would like to expand and develop. You may even decide that you need to digress for a while, in order to strengthen a weakness.
- **Congratulate yourself** – When you have achieved a target, or completed a stage on the way to your overall goal, remember to notice it and congratulate yourself. Tell yourself how well you are doing and reward yourself in some way. It's tempting to think that the achievement itself is the reward, but our minds don't always seem to work in that way – we want recognition and celebration as well.

Turn negative labels into positive ones.
We all have our strengths and weaknesses, but people with resilient self-confidence and high self-esteem are often able to recognize that there are positive sides even to 'undesirable' traits.

We frequently judge ourselves too harshly, giving negative

labels to aspects of our character that others would view more positively.

Think what labels you might have given yourself and decide what *other* words you could use to describe that trait. Many 'faults' have a much more favourable description that could help you to think about, and develop, positive qualities.

Thinking about yourself more generously helps you to work *with* your character, rather than against it. Understanding your potential allows development of greater self-esteem and self-confidence.

If you always think of yourself as bossy, for example, you may see this trait as negative and try to play it down. In doing so, you may not notice that it is this characteristic that encourages you to take charge and be responsible for things. By changing the way you label yourself from 'bossy' to 'responsible', you free yourself to concentrate on finding ways to express your aptitude for responsibility effectively and diplomatically.

Negative label	Positive label
Lazy	Relaxed
Fussy	Attentive to detail
Stubborn	Persistent
Aggressive	Determined
Rude	Forthright
Shy	Sensitive
Bossy	Responsible
Timid	Cautious
Stuffy	Formal
Old-fashioned	Traditional
Loud	Enthusiastic

Turn negative talk into positive talk
Give your confidence a chance to grow by stopping the

self-critical talk that we all tend to indulge in at times.

We are often our own harshest critics, and our thoughts about ourselves can be very unkind. We wouldn't let anyone else talk to us in this way.

Frequent criticism saps self-confidence and makes it difficult to experiment or take risks in case of mistakes. Replace your negative comments and judgements about your own behaviour with more objective ones that allow you to learn from the experience and try again.

When you catch yourself making negative remarks about yourself or your performance, stop and think what the humane version would be.

Negative statements	**Positive statements**
I can't do this	This will take time and concentration
I did something terrible	I made a mistake
I'm a clumsy idiot	I tripped over
I'm no good	I'm OK
I *must* do better	I could improve by doing it differently
I ought to try harder	I'm doing really well in the circumstances
They won't like me	They'll think I'm OK

Appear confident
If you behave confidently others will treat you as if you are confident, and, eventually, you will actually become confident.

Behaving in a confident manner is a good way to start *feeling* confident, just as behaving in a timid, hesitant way might start to make you feel less self-assured.

SOFT

An easy way to appear confident, friendly, and approachable is to take the SOFT option. This stands for:

Smile	Smile and look cheerful – other people will respond to you positively.
Open	Use 'open' rather than 'closed' postures. For example, instead of folding your arms, which looks defensive, rest your hands on your lap or on the arm of the chair. Similarly, instead of hugging a file or a bag to your chest, put it down and let your arms relax. Hold your head up instead of letting it sink down into your collar.
Forward	Look forward, lean forward. In other words, make eye contact with the person you are speaking to, don't back away from them. Face them and clearly direct your attention towards them.
Touch	Practise giving a firm handshake, and offer it confidently.

3
SECURITY

WHAT IS SECURITY?
A dictionary definition of secure is: '*Untroubled by danger or fear, certain not to fail or give way or be lost.*'

The key word is *untroubled*. This doesn't mean that danger or fear are unknown, but that they are not unduly threatening. Someone who feels secure isn't overcome by nameless dread, nor do they find uncertainty unbearable.

The secure are self-reliant in the knowledge that they can trust themselves and their resources.

They have usually been put to the test before, and found that they survived. From past experience they are, therefore, reasonably sure that they will survive this time as well.

Security is the ability to be flexible and adapt to change. The opposite of security is insecurity. Someone who feels insecure lacks this central core of self-reliance and is unable to respond flexibly and creatively to change.

Fear and apprehension underpin insecurity and hold it in place. This is usually a mixture of some or all of the following basic fears:

Fear of disruption Change threatens the plans that we have made for ourselves and our lives. We are no longer sure if the goals that we have set for ourselves are attainable in this new situation. Our sense of personal direction becomes uncertain.

Fear of loss When things change, there is no absolute guarantee that anything that we rely on or value will remain. There is no certainty that change will bring improvement; in fact, in the case of redundancy, the change will almost certainly, at least in the short term, be for the worse.

Fear of demands It will take time, energy and effort to understand this new situation, and we may not be sure we have the resources. The skills and experience that we have worked hard to acquire may be of no use to us in this new situation.

Fear of loss of power We may not be sure anymore just how much this new situation is under our control. It may feel as if outside forces have swept away our own autonomy. We may fear losing our footing and being swept helplessly away.

Job security, at least for the foreseeable future, may be very difficult to come by. Those people who can find security within themselves, and from what they find around them, are in a markedly better position than those who rely on their work to give them stability.

WHY DOES REBUILDING SECURITY HELP?
Redundancy and unemployment bring major changes that often seem to threaten the stability of our lives.

They affect our sense of security in those major areas where security is important to us. It is desirable, therefore, to deal positively with the feelings of insecurity that may come up by consciously rebuilding and strengthening our safety and stability in whatever way we can.

Stability and security are important to us as human beings, they are fundamental to our well-being. When we have them, we have a solid base from which to deal with what is happening. We don't consequently become fearful of change and try to avoid it. When things outside our control force change upon us, we believe we can rely on our inner resources. We can be flexible in our response, and cope with it well.

A solid, inner, well-founded sense of security will help you to cope successfully with the changes happening around you. Moreover, it may help you to actually take advantage of those changes.

People with little sense of security may find themselves overwhelmed by the feelings of insecurity brought about by job loss.

These may induce worry and alarm about circumstances and future prospects. Their actions may, consequently, become panic-stricken, unfocused and produce little result. Poor results induce even greater insecurity, along with increased worry and panic. Behaviour becomes even more random, frenzied, and unproductive. And so it goes on.

The areas of life where security is often found to be of most importance to people are:

- Friends and family
- Money
- Personal skills and talents

People who take active steps to rebuild their sense of security in these areas after a crisis such as redundancy, survive much better than those who don't. They are often found to:

- Be less stressed about enforced changes.
- Adapt to circumstances better.
- Be more flexible about future plans and expectations.
- Find job hunting less stressful.
- Take better advantage of opportunities.
- Cope better with uncertainty.
- Regard themselves positively.

REBUILDING SECURITY: WHAT TO DO
Redundancy and unemployment can constitute a severe threat to feelings of stability and safety. You need to strengthen your security in those areas where it is especially important:

- **Friends and family** – Build, repair, and maintain your social support networks.
- **Money** – Work out your finances and adapt your lifestyle accordingly.
- **Personal skills and talents** – Assess your qualities, adapt and expand them.

FRIENDS AND FAMILY – BUILDING SUPPORT
One of the most important sources of stability, security and support for the majority of people is the network of family and friends they have built around them over the years.

Redundancy can be a threat to this network. The worry, stress, low self-esteem and depression that may accompany some stages of your adaptation to changed circumstances, can often lead to isolation and loneliness if you begin to avoid people.

Those who survive redundancy well, take steps to ensure that they strengthen their ties with family and friends at this time. They are also pragmatic, though, about what to expect from human nature. They accept that some friends will cope less easily with *their* change of circumstances, than others.

There are things that you specifically need to do to reinforce your links with others at this time:

Tell them what has happened
This can be the hardest part, but if you want to give your family and your friends the opportunity to support you through this crisis, you need to let them know what has happened.

It is no good pretending that nothing has occurred, that everything is still the same. This will not only undermine your security, it will undermine theirs as well. They will know that you are different, and will wonder what the matter is.

Tell people as straightforwardly as possible, but remember that for some it will come as a shock. Partners and children, especially, need to be told frankly but be prepared for people to be upset or angry, particularly if your redundancy affects them personally. Give them time to come to terms with it.

Sometimes, shock may cause those that you tell to behave insensitively or embarrassingly. Be tolerant and give them the benefit of the doubt until they've had time to get over it. Don't let it affect your own self-esteem, though – their reactions are their responsibility, not yours.

Include them

Partners and children, in particular, will be involved in your redundancy. There is little point in trying 'not to worry them'. Discuss what has happened and what it will mean to you all. Their future has been affected as well; they may have negative thoughts and feelings to deal with. You need to include them in any planning or decision-making that you do.

You need to:

- Listen to their views and opinions
- Ask their advice
- Let them know what they can do to assist

Friends are often anxious to help but don't know what to do. If there *is* some way they can help, then ask them clearly. It's easy to be resentful because someone doesn't do something, even though we haven't *actually* asked them if they will.

Friends can help by:

- Listening
- Offering advice from their own experience
- Coaching – reading through our CVs, going through mock interviews
- Telling you what you do well
- Helping you put things in perspective

Do things together
Actively make time for family and friends. Get in contact with people, face to face or over the phone, and give them some of your time and attention. Plan activities together, have fun, get to know them better, and strengthen your lines of communication.

Find other sources of support
Although family and friends are of immense importance during this time, it is unfair to expect them to shoulder the entire burden and be unfailingly supportive. It helps everybody to build a greater sense of security if you look for as many sources of help as possible.

Two specific sources you could consider are:

- *Unemployment support and self-help groups* – Find out what is available in your area from the Citizens Advice Bureau, the Department of Employment, or a library. There may be groups set up in your workplace, if a number of you are being made redundant; alternatively you may set up your own. They largely provide a place to meet and share problems, advice, and support.
- *Job clubs* – These are open to you after six months of unemployment. They provide job-search advice and all the facilities you need such as: photocopying, word-processing, postage, newspapers, journals and

telephones. Fellow members also provide company and moral support. Find out what is available through the Department of Employment.

MONEY

Managing finances

One of the things that people who cope well with redundancy and unemployment do is to make sure that they *actively* manage their finances. This can be difficult in the circumstances as it might be tempting to think it will be less stressful not to know what is happening to your bank account.

It can also be tempting to console yourself with morale-boosting treats from any lump sum that you may have received. It's often best, though, to give yourself time to adjust before undertaking any major financial commitments.

Increase your overall security by studying, and coming to terms with, your financial situation. Work out what you have and what you are going to need.

Find out what you're entitled to

There is a full range of benefits, concessions and rebates available to you when you become unemployed. Find out what you are entitled to right from your very first day of unemployment – contact your local Employment Office to make an appointment with an adviser.

Knowing exactly what you will be getting over the long term will help you to decide how to balance your budget. You will be more sure about what you can afford, and how you need to adapt your living patterns to adjust to your expected income.

Work out your budget

Having found out exactly what your income is going to be, work out how much you can afford to spend. Consider if you want to add regularly to your income from savings or any redundancy lump sum that you may have.

It is enormously helpful to have the figures down in black and white so that you can get a picture of your finances and juggle them around as necessary.

Draw up a list of *all* your monthly outgoings. This will include essentials like mortgage or rent, gas and electricity, food, telephone, etc. It should also include non-essentials such as entertainment, clothes, magazines, etc. Against each one, write down how much you currently spend on it, and how much you intend to spend in the future. There may be outgoings that you can substantially reduce, or even drop, for the time being. Adjust the figures until income and outgoings match each other.

Example

Item	Current Cost	Future Cost	Change?
mortgage	£150.00	£150.00	none
electricity	£20.00	£15.00	be more careful, improve insulation
food	£120.00	£80.00	switch to own-brands
telephone	£30.00	£30.00	none – I need to be in contact
clothes	£150.00	£20.00	stick to repairs and essentials
entertainment	£120.00	£40.00	improvise!
child care	£95.00	£0.00	not necessary at present
miscellaneous	£20.00	£20.00	need to build in some reserve
Total	£705.00	£355.00	

Once you know how much you intend to spend on each item, stick to it. If you have problems keeping within the limit for a particular item, keep on trying for at least a couple of months. Wait until you can see if you have genuinely set the level too low, or if you just need time to adapt.

PERSONAL SKILLS AND TALENTS

Assessing your qualities

Those who come through redundancy successfully are often found to have very clear ideas of exactly what their skills and qualities are. This helps both indirectly – by helping them maintain their self-respect and self-esteem, and directly – by enabling them to be flexible and creative about the sort of work they are looking for.

Many will also have actively added to those skills during their period of unemployment, so increasing their self-confidence and their value in the workplace.

They have a sense of what their strengths and weaknesses are. They are able to take advantage of strengths, and take steps to correct or modify weaknesses where they are a disadvantage.

Increase your security by assessing exactly what your personal characteristics are:

- Look at your skills
- Look at your qualities
- Look at your strengths
- Look at your weaknesses

Look at your skills

Our skills are our knowledge and abilities. Often, though not always, we have to learn the skills to begin with and then practise them in order to improve them. Driving or typing are two examples that show this very clearly – we have to be taught how to drive initially, and, after we've grasped the basics, practice increases competence.

Other skills, like reading, are taught at a very young age and we become reasonably competent at them early on. There are some, like communication skills, that we all learn naturally and have a basic ability with. At a basic level we can all understand others and make ourselves understood, but we can significantly improve this ability at a later stage if we wish.

People who come through redundancy well, often place an equal value on *all* their skills, not just the job-related ones. They will see their parenting skills, for example, as being as important as their workplace ones. They may value the skills they developed through a hobby such as music or sport as highly as those developed at work.

This means that, when they are out of work, their value of themselves doesn't drop as dramatically as those whose value is completely tied up with their job. They still have plenty of opportunities to exercise skills they feel are important.

Look at what your abilities are over the wider range of your life. Think about all the things that you do, and all the times and places where you exercise different skills:

work	concerns
home	interests
leisure	pursuits
hobbies	as a parent
as a partner	with friends
study	with family
sports	on your own
crafts	for fun

Write down all the skills that you use to carry out each of these activities. Some skills will be with people, some will be with things, others will be with ideas. Most activities will demand a mixture of skills. Here are some examples:

organizing	driving
making	crafting
delegating	managing
communicating	planning
presenting	innovating
studying	computing
repairing	typing
specifying	leading
listening	building
writing	supervising
counselling	travelling
teaching	creating
accounting	observing
budgeting	reporting
campaigning	analyzing
fund-raising	influencing
negotiating	selling
motivating	trading

Congratulate yourself on the number of skills that you exercise in your everyday life. Think about which of these skills you value and are important to you. Look at each of your skills in turn and decide whether:

- You want to improve or strengthen it in any way
- You want to add to it in any way
- You would like to use it more often
- You are happy with it as it is

Example

Skill	What to do with it
communication	*use more often* – try skills with kids instead of shouting at them
language	*add to* – join conversational Spanish class for holiday use
typing	*improve* – enter for RSA qualification, practise to improve speed
observing	*do nothing* – happy with it as it is

List the things that you want to do, such as finding a Spanish class and registering for the RSA exam in the above example. Think about the steps you will need to take in order to do anything about it. You may need to ring the local college, drop in at the adult education centre, or decide what to cut back on in order to fit it in. Plan how, when, and where you will actually carry out these steps.

Look at your qualities

Qualities are the facets of your personality that you have developed throughout your life. Like skills, we may have basic qualities that we can develop further as the need or the occasion arises.

Also, as with skills, it is more helpful to look at your qualities over the broader range of your life, rather than just concentrating on those that are more relevant to work.

List the qualities that you recognize within yourself. Here are some examples:

kindness	ambition
intelligence	dependability
responsibility	flexibility
leadership	versatility
understanding	perception
friendliness	diplomacy
wit	sensitivity
punctuality	practicality
imagination	honesty
determination	persistence
unflappability	energy
efficiency	patience

Congratulate yourself on the number of qualities that you possess. Think about which of these qualities you value and are important to you. Look at each of your qualities in turn and decide whether:

- You want to improve or strengthen it in any way

- You want to add to it in any way
- You would like to use it more often
- You are happy with it as it is

Example

Quality	What to do with it
flexibility	*use more often* – try new ways of doing things instead of the usual
efficiency	*improve* – find time-management course or self-help book
punctuality	*add to* – pick up new bus and train timetables, get watch repaired
honesty	*do nothing* – happy with it as it is

List the things that you want to do. Think about the steps you will need to take in order to do anything about it. Plan how, and when, and where you will actually carry out these steps.

Look at your strengths

Your strengths are the things that you are good at, the things that you feel confident about doing. They are a mixture of skills and qualities that you value and can use with assurance.

Write down the things that you do well, that are your strengths, and list all the skills and qualities that go with that activity.

Example

I am good at	skills needed	qualities needed
organizing community newsletter	typing, organizing, design, communication, negotiation	tact, responsibility, versatility, imagination, wit
cooking meals	planning, budgeting, making, supervising, timing	imagination, patience, energy, practicality
teaching music	musical, teaching, organizing, communication, listening, motivating	friendliness, discipline, understanding, patience, persistence

Think about your strengths. Are there skills that you could add, or qualities that you could develop, that would further enhance your strong points?

If there are, what steps do you need to achieve this?

Look at your weaknesses

As you list your strengths, you may come across skills or qualities that you feel are important in this particular activity, but which you feel you don't have, or which you have not particularly developed – these are your weaknesses.

For instance, in the above example, the quality of patience might be important to teaching music. If you lacked this particular quality or it was only weakly developed in you, you would probably want to do something about it.

Similarly, a knowledge of nutrition might be an important skill to someone who cooks family meals. It would greatly enhance this 'strength' to be able to add this particular skill.

Take note of any weaknesses you may have and decide whether:

- You want to improve on it
- You can get around it or compensate for it
- It's not that important

Example

Weakness	What to do about it
versatility	*improve it* – practise thinking of different ways of doing things before deciding which option
public speaking	*improve it* – find practical course or self-help books, practise with friends to improve confidence
leadership	*compensate* – use communication skills and qualities of understanding and patience instead
study skills	*do nothing* – it's not that important at the moment

PERFECT REDUNDANCY

List the things that you want to do.

Think about the steps you will need to take in order to do anything about it.

Plan how, when, and where you will actually carry them out.

4
GOALS

WHAT ARE GOALS
Goals are intentions. They are a statement about what you want to do, what you intend to achieve.

A goal is an end result, a destination, the place that you are aiming for. We achieve goals through a series of actions or tasks, and many goals will have a number of targets leading up to them.

Example
We may have the goal of going away on holiday. In order to achieve this, we would need to set a number of targets, and undertake a series of actions.

Our targets, for example, might be – choose a destination; find the right holiday at the right price; book the holiday with the travel agent in good time, and so on.

To achieve our first target, we would need to take actions such as collecting holiday brochures, assessing finances, getting ideas of preferences, having a family discussion.

Having achieved our first target, we can move on to our second, working steadily towards our goal – the best holiday we can get, at a price that we can afford.

Goals provide the motivation we need in order to do anything. It is quite hard to get started on something unless we have some idea of why we are doing it and what we hope to achieve. Virtually everything that we do has a reason and an aim – an outcome that we desire.

Sometimes this aim is obscure and complicated, even to

ourselves, but most of the time it is relatively simple and straightforward. By consciously setting clear, well-defined goals we can choose the simplest, most effective route for getting there.

We not only need to know *what* we intend to do, we need to know *why* we are doing it. We need to base our goals on our own personal values. If goals are to motivate us to do things, we have to feel that what we will achieve is important to us.

We can, to some extent, be driven by the 'carrot and stick' principle — a series of rewards and punishments usually designed to make us carry out someone else's aims and objectives. But we achieve a higher degree of satisfaction when we set our own goals, based on our own values and following our own priorities.

By thinking about what we want, and setting clear goals to achieve, we gain responsibility and self-control in our lives — self-determination. We get to know what our own personal values and priorities are, and can plan our lives in ways that are consistent with them.

We can stay in tune with our own aims and ideals, take realistic steps to put them into practice and make them a reality.

People who don't set goals run the risk of letting others set the agenda, and finding the values and priorities that they believe in are largely neglected.

WHY DOES SETTING GOALS HELP?

People who survive redundancy and unemployment and come out of it with a positive attitude towards themselves, are often found to be very good at setting personal goals.

They set clear, well-defined goals over a wide area of their lives, not just in the area relating to work. They have many objectives over a range of endeavours and interests.

This means that unemployment, while necessitating a change of targets in one part of their life, often has little adverse effect on the other major areas. They continue to work steadily towards the objectives that they have set themselves in other spheres.

This way, they retain a sense of onward momentum rather than stagnation. Despite the circumstances, they continue, at some level, to look for a steady improvement in their quality of life. There seems to be a decision, consciously or unconsciously, that if the improvement in, say, material quality has been blocked temporarily, they will redirect their efforts towards improvement in other areas. This may be in their self-development, relationships, creativity or education – whatever is important to them.

Although finding another job is an important goal – probably a high-priority category 'A' goal into which they direct a great deal of time and effort – it is not their *only* goal. They consequently avoid making too big an emotional commitment to their job search, and are spared the debilitating extremes of hope and despair that often accompany it.

In working towards personal goals based on personal values, people are significantly more likely to take calculated risks and stretch themselves in order to achieve them. They are also more likely to add new skills and develop their personal qualities as a result. This has a clearly beneficial effect on self-esteem and self-confidence.

People who set themselves personal goals are more likely to:

- Be clear about their values and priorities

- Retain their sense of identity
- Have a wider view of what they want to achieve
- Be more flexible about the route they take towards it
- Retain their self-worth
- Have more creative strategies
- Get less bogged down in meaningless tasks
- Retain their motivation
- Report better levels of overall satisfaction

When we relate our actions to an overall goal instead of undertaking a series of meaningless tasks, we are more likely to remain motivated and on top of things.

We are also more likely to make effective plans and take rational decisions in pursuit of our objective. We can be flexible and creative about how we actually achieve each goal. There is usually more than one route, and often many paths, to an objective. This gives us many more options about how we achieve a particular outcome.

SETTING GOALS: WHAT TO DO

To set attainable goals you need to:

- Assess your values
- Define your goals
- Plan your actions

Assess your values

Before you can begin to define your goals, it is helpful to know what your values, ideals, and beliefs are. It is on these that you will base satisfying objectives.

Everybody has their own unique set of values and priorities that are built up over a lifetime. Only you can say what is important to you.

Think about, identify and tick any of the following that you value in the various areas of your life, add any others that occur to you:

Relationships – What is important to you in your relationships with other people? What do you value in your relationships with your friends, partner, or family?

trust		honesty	
love		having a good time	
closeness		casualness	
shared interests		a few close friends	
shared rituals		lots of friends	
quality time		knowing you belong	
openness		shared intimacy	
being needed		close family ties	
commitment		freedom	
unspoken understanding		physical attractiveness	
political beliefs			

Home – What is important to you about your home environment? What do you value about your house, the atmosphere in your home?

privacy		light	
tranquillity		freshness	
cosiness		warmth	
cleanliness		comfort	
stimulation		personal possessions	
liveliness		surroundings	
security		own front door	
personal expression		good taste	
open house		freedom	

Work – What is it that is important to you about your work? What do you value about it? Possibilities might include some of the following:

PERFECT REDUNDANCY

responsibility		demanding	
challenge		easy	
being valued		part of a team	
highly ethical		creativity	
praise		variety	
interesting		close to home	
stimulating		lots of travelling	
fast track		meeting people	
working with ideas		being involved	
self-expression		low stress	
pleasant environment		self directed	
power		good workmates	

Personal development – What is it that is important to you about your development as a person? What do you value about yourself?

health		social relationships	
creativity		spiritual growth	
knowledge		specific skills	
artistry		talents	
status		physical appearance	
personality		sexuality	
role in society		ethics	
strength		fitness	
sensitivity		dexterity	

Finance – What is it that is important to you financially and materially? What do you value about money and goods?

security		investment	
value		a good address	
status		self-respect	
comfort		generosity	
freedom		indulgence	
respectability		choice	
having a good time		a good pension	
adequate insurance		power	
freedom from drudgery		provision for children	

Other – What is it that is important to you that you haven't covered yet? What other areas of your life do you value?

community		history	
politics		gender	
religion		environment	
ethnicity		therapy	
wishes		dreams	
fantasies		social commitment	

DEFINE YOUR GOALS

Once you know what is important to you, you can start to define your goals within each area.

Taking each area in turn, look at your values and think about what you would like to achieve in that sphere.

Example

Relationship goals
- Establish better relationship with neighbours
- Develop more interests with partner
- Spend more time with Debbie
- Be more understanding to Paul
- Get close to the children

Home goals
- Make bedroom tranquil haven
- Insulate loft
- Get the garden in order
- Make kitchen more cheerful
- Keep everything tidier
- Make space for hobbies

Career goals
- Bring training up to date
- Get job more involved with people
- Get experience working with technology
- Socialize with colleagues in future
- Aspire to management position

Financial goals
- Start pension plan
- Invest time rather than money in things
- Save each week to go out Saturday night
- Follow stock market
- Maximize interest payments

Personal development goals
- Improve health
- Take up piano again
- Relax more
- Be more alert to opportunities

Other goals
- Get more involved with the community
- Campaign for better bus services
- Become school governor
- Fund-raise for hospital

SMARTS
Once you have an idea what your goals are, you can select the ones that attract you the most at present, and begin to define them more clearly.

To ensure that they are clear, well thought out, and well defined, goals need to be:

Specific	Vague goals are no use, keep them concrete, simple, and direct. If a goal seems complicated when you put it into words, maybe you need to break it down into two or three simpler goals.
Measurable	You need to include some way of knowing how you are progressing, and also of knowing very clearly when you have reached your goal.
Achievable	Keep goals realistic, don't aim impossibly high. If you reach this goal, you can always set another, more challenging one afterwards.
Result-based	Write your goals in terms of what you intend to achieve. For example: 'Go to the gym' is an action. It isn't really a goal because it doesn't state what you intend to achieve by going to the gym. The goal might be something like, 'Improve muscular strength' – this would be what you aim to achieve.
Time-tabled	Include some idea for yourself of when you want to achieve your goal by, and how long you expect it to take. This will give you a framework when you come to plan your actions.
Supported	Include an idea of what support you could use, who could help, how, and when.

This takes some time to do, but it is well worth it in the long run.

You should now have several very clearly defined goals. These may be major, life-defining objectives, or simpler, practical intentions.

PLAN YOUR ACTIONS

For each goal, think about the actions that you will have to undertake to achieve it. Consider any targets that you might set as smaller steps to your main goal, if this will make planning easier.

Example

Home environment

Value: Peace and quiet

Goal: I will clear out and redecorate the small back bedroom by the end of the month for use as a 'quiet room' for reading, away from the television

Targets: Clear out room by end of next week
Redecorate by end of month

Action: Explain to family and get support, clear space in garage for storage, sort out junk, look in attic for suitable furniture, pictures, etc., buy paint, save newspapers to protect the floor, find and clean brushes and rollers, etc., check DIY books for tips and ideas.

When you have long-term goals, it is extremely helpful to plan the targets between where you are now and where you want to be. You will then have a series of short steps rather than one big jump between you and your goal:

- Start with your final goal and work backwards
- Ask yourself where you would need to be, what experience, qualifications, etc. you would need to have in order to be able to step straight into your goal. (If you don't know, find out.)
  →This is your *'minus one'* target.
- Ask yourself where you would need to be, what experience, qualifications, etc. you would need to have in order to be able to step straight into your 'minus one' target.
  →This is your *'minus two'* target.
- Ask yourself where you would need to be, what experience, qualifications, etc. you would need to have in order to be able to step straight into your 'minus two' target.
  →This is your *'minus three'* target.
- Continue until you arrive back at the position where you are now.

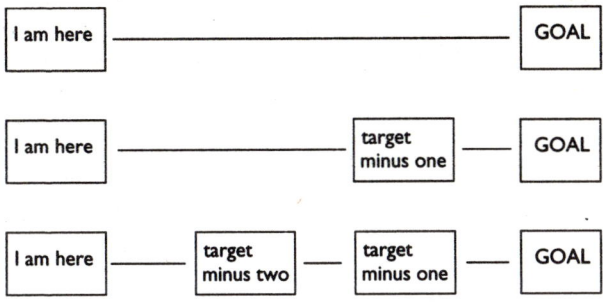

Example

At the moment, I am involved in catering sales, but my ambition has always been to set up my own business as a high-quality confectioner specializing in the gourmet market.

So, what sort of person becomes a quality, specialist confectioner? A good bet would be someone who was already a chief confectioner with an outstanding company, who had a network of contacts, and a really good reputation from winning various prestigious prizes.

So how do I become this person? One way would be to work my way there from a good company with a good reputation who offered further training. I could take specialist courses outside work as well. And a good way to start winning competitions is to enter them at a junior level and work my way up.

So how do I get started? To get into a good company I need some experience with the manufacture of confectionery. To get experience, I first need to have some training before anyone will employ me.

So what's my first step? Enrol at catering college.

Goal	Set up own business as high-quality specialist confectioner
Target *minus one:*	Chief confectioner with high-profile quality employer. Network of contacts. Good reputation from competitions.
Target *minus two:*	Confectioner with quality company. Further specialist training. Enter competitions – get name known.
Target *minus three:*	Experience with reputable confectionery company.
Target *minus four:*	Confectionery course at catering college.
I am here:	Working part-time in catering sales.

Now I only need to work out the actions necessary to achieve each target. To reach the first target – target minus four – for example, I might need to contact colleges, get hold of prospectuses, work out finances, etc.

Once I am well on my way to achieving this first target, I can start thinking about what actions I need to take to achieve my next target.

For example, once I am at college doing the catering course, my actions for achieving target minus three might be to read trade journals, find out more about the confectionery business, visit companies, get a CV together, arrange holiday work-placements, etc.

Using this method, it is possible to break down seemingly impossible goals into simple steps.

Part Two:
THINGS THAT MAY GET IN THE WAY

This section looks at the negative emotions that you may encounter, and which may get in the way of you achieving a constructive recovery from redundancy.

These can be summed up as:

- **Stress**

- **Worry**

- **Anger**

- **Apathy**

- **Depression**

Each chapter first describes each of these states, suggests why it might arise during redundancy and unemployment, and then goes on to look at effective ways of coping with it.

5
STRESS

WHAT IS STRESS:
Our bodies have excellent ways of dealing with dangerous or threatening situations. When alarmed or threatened they are designed to *either*:

- stay and fight whatever is threatening us

or

- run away from the danger

In order to do one or other of the above, we undergo all sorts of physical and chemical changes – this is referred to as the 'fight or flight' response.

This way of dealing with danger worked very well in the past – human beings wouldn't be around now if it didn't. Unfortunately, we developed them when the things that were likely to be dangerous or threatening were relatively uncomplicated – a sabre-toothed tiger or a charging rhino, for example.

Unhappily, many of the things that threaten us these days are more complicated and less clear-cut. They are actually more difficult to deal with, and neither staying and fighting nor running away is the right, or the best, thing to do.

As a result our bodies become confused about how to respond and what to respond to. The result is that we are continually half-prepared for 'fight or flight', and all sorts of flustered and bewildering chemical messages are produced inside us.

SYMPTOMS OF STRESS

If this half-prepared state goes on for any length of time, our bodies can't rest or relax properly and our ability to react appropriately to situations becomes lessened. Additionally, the continued physical and chemical changes to our bodies take their toll on our health and well-being. Eventually, this adds up to what we recognize as 'stress'.

Depending on the individual concerned the symptoms of stress are many and varied. Some early warning signals to watch out for, though, include:

Physical symptoms

headaches	constipation or diarrhoea
indigestion	palpitations
frequent heartburn	chest pains
insomnia	tics or twitches
change of appetite	excessive sweating
constant tiredness	impotence or frigidity

Emotional symptoms

difficulty relaxing	poor concentration
irritability	loss of humour
short temper	frequent desire to cry
indecision	anxiety
loss of attention	

WHY MIGHT YOU FEEL STRESSED?

Stress is most likely to happen when we have, or *feel that we have*, little or no control over what is happening to us. We feel stressed when we are battling to gain control over situations without much certainty of success, or when we feel trapped in a situation we can't change.

Stress also happens when we are under the wrong amount of or the wrong *kind* of pressure. Being under pressure when we feel we are working towards a goal and achieving something feels very different from when we are under pressure but achieving nothing and fearing failure.

Unemployment can make us feel trapped in a situation that is outside our control, facing all the wrong sorts of pressure:

The Stress of Change
All change is stressful to a greater or lesser extent. Even when the change is welcome, we still have to adapt to it mentally and physically. When the change is unwelcome, adapting to it can be very hard indeed.

Unemployment causes a great many changes to happen at once. Routines, expectations, plans and relationships may alter radically.

There is also stress about the uncertainty of future change. How, when, and where will another job be forthcoming? What will happen in the meantime?

Work Stress
A great deal of pressure and uncertainty may occur while still at work – rumours and stories about redundancy before anything is officially known; a tense waiting period while everybody wonders 'Will it be me?'; further waves of redundancy when everything seemed settled.

Working in an atmosphere like this for any length of time can leave a residue of stress that makes it harder to find the resources to cope when redundancy is finally confirmed.

Family and Relationship Stress
Becoming unemployed can alter the balance in family relationships. Even just being at home instead of work can cause problems.

Conflicts and difficulties between partners, or parents and children can arise because of worry, uncertainty and disappointment. This then causes more stress and even more conflict.

Financial Stress
Financial change is often very stressful. Having too little money causes obvious problems. Having too much, if there is a generous redundancy settlement, can cause worry too – what's the best way to invest it? How can I make it last longer? What should I do with it?

Emotional Stress
Redundancy and unemployment can cause a lot of negative emotions such as anxiety, shame, guilt, fear and grief. These can be hard to express and, consequently, churn around inside us adding to the stress of the situation.

OVERCOMING STRESS: WHAT TO DO ABOUT IT
There is a lot of help and advice around about dealing with stress in general. Leaflets, books and booklets should be readily available from libraries, doctors' surgeries, and larger chemists' shops, as well as bookshops, specialist health shops and health centres.

For help with the stress of unemployment in particular, follow as much of the advice as possible in *Part One: Things that help:*

- Maintain as many as possible of the structures and benefits that you formerly achieved through paid work
- Take steps to build up your self-confidence and self-worth
- Maintain your contacts and social links
- Think positively and channel your energy productively
- Set realistic goals for yourself
- Treat yourself well
- Get some support
- Update your skills and develop your education

If, however, stress itself is preventing you from doing this, the following self-help methods may be useful.

If at any time you suspect that the stress you are feeling may be too much for you to deal with on your own, then go and see your doctor. Doctors are used to treating stress and have the experience, training, and resources to help you.

Relax
What is relaxation? What does being relaxed feel like?

Physical signs
slow pulse rate	muscles heavy	slow, deep breathing
slow heartbeat	muscles relaxed	breathing from stomach

Emotional signs
feeling unhurried	sense of peace	sense of space
feeling unpressured	feeling open	sense of openness
feeling calm	clarity of thought	

You have probably noticed that these signs are the opposite of the tense, tight and pressured feelings associated with being stressed.

Getting relaxed
Take time each day to practise consciously relaxing, both physically and mentally.

Physical relaxation
The best and easiest way to relax tension in your muscles is to deliberately tense and relax each group of muscles in turn:

1 Sit or lie in a quiet, comfortable place where you won't be disturbed.
2 Begin by taking a deep breath in and letting it out slowly.
3 Just enjoy letting go and breathing quietly for a

moment.
4   Thinking of your feet first, tense the muscles in your feet for a second or two and then let go and release the tension.
5   Tense the muscles in your legs for a second or two and then let go.
6   Continue all the way up your body, tensing and releasing your muscles.
7   Finally, squeeze your face muscles up into a tight grimace and then let go and relax.
8   Remain quietly relaxed for a few moments breathing slowly and gently.

Mental relaxation

This exercise can continue on from the previous one while you're lying quietly relaxed, or you can do it separately if you wish.
1   Make yourself comfortable
2   Close your eyes and remember, or imagine, a place that is ideal for relaxing – on the beach, perhaps, or a peaceful summer garden.
3   Imagine that you are actually in this tranquil place – explore and enjoy all the sights and sounds and scents around you. Feel the sun warm on your skin; hear the gentle waves or the soft rustling of leaves.
4   If any tense thoughts intrude, simply accept them and then let go of them. Bring your thoughts back to the peaceful place you are imagining.
5   Enjoy the peace and the calmness.
6   After five or ten minutes, open your eyes. Take a deep breath and let it out slowly.
7   Have a good stretch. Sit up or get up in your own time.

Each of these exercises can be completed within five to ten minutes, if that's all the time you can spare. Otherwise, take as long as you like.

Many people find that listening to relaxing music or a recording of appropriate natural sounds, helps the exercises along. This can also be useful if you worry about how long you've been relaxing and whether you might drop off to sleep – you tend to wake up automatically when the sound stops.

Staying relaxed
As well as getting relaxed and practising relaxation on a regular basis, develop the habit of staying relaxed throughout the day:

- Take time, every so often, to check for tensed muscle – hunched shoulders, habitual frown, tense stomach, etc. – and consciously let those muscles relax.
- Check your breathing as well. If it feels shallow and laboured, take a deep breath to relax your chest and let it out slowly.
- Take moderate exercise. This needn't be anything elaborate, just a simple fifteen or twenty minute walk every day will help work off tension. Wear comfortable clothes and shoes.
- Eat well and eat wisely. A healthy, balanced diet – which also includes things you enjoy – helps your body to undo the effects of stress.
- Go easy with the things that can put extra stress on your body:
    - caffeine in tea, coffee and cola drinks
    - chocolate, sweets and sugar
    - junk food
    - cigarettes
    - alcohol
- Do things that give you pleasure.
- Spend time with people who appreciate you.

Being stressed uses up the valuable physical and emotional resources needed to deal with unemployment.

PERFECT REDUNDANCY

By staying calm and relaxed you will have the energy to deal with things, and will be able to think and plan constructively.

6
WORRY

WHAT IS WORRY?
Worry is often an aspect of stress. It's included separately, though, as it is quite possible to worry without being stressed. There are also ways of dealing with worry that deserve a space to themselves.

Worry can be defined as that sense of fear and apprehension that we feel when we are anxious about things or events that are neither within our control, nor have a clear-cut outcome.

The techniques that we normally use for solving problems don't seem to work as well for the things that we worry about. Instead of being able either to do something about them, or to forget them, the worry just sits there.

We know we have a problem, and we know that we haven't yet solved it. But our thoughts keep returning to it. Each time it looks more difficult to solve. The more we think about it, the more complicated it appears. The more this happens, the more we worry.

SYMPTOMS OF WORRY
When we worry, we return again and again to a particular subject without ever achieving anything constructive. Often the problem seems to get worse *because* we keep coming back to it without any resolution.

Worry, like stress, uses up the precious resources that we really should be devoting to coping with unemployment.

While we are worrying in this way, our minds are not free to deal effectively with our real problems.

Physical symptoms

insomnia	comfort eating
fidgeting	change of appetite
nervous mannerisms	'gnawing' in stomach
biting lips or nails	inability to relax
smoking more	tension headache

Mental symptoms

difficulty concentrating	sense of dread
same thoughts going round	loss of other interests
keep returning to same subject	feelings of indecision
loss of perspective	anxious dreams or nightmares
loss of humour	distraction

WHY MIGHT YOU FEEL WORRIED?

Being unemployed provides fertile ground for things to worry about. A lot of things change at the same time, much of it feels out of our control, and the outcome is often uncertain.

The sort of things that we often worry about when we become unemployed includes:

Finance
- Will I have enough money to live on?
- Will I be able to afford things for my family and myself?
- What happens if I can't pay the bills?
- What will our living conditions be like and will be they unbearable?
- How do I deal with the bureaucracy to get benefits and what if I get it wrong?

Future prospects
- Do I have the ability or the energy to start again?
- Will I ever get anywhere?
- What if I'm unemployable?
- What is the point of my life and where am I going?
- What have I achieved so far, anyway?

Applying for jobs
- What do they want from me and how do I know what to put in the application?
- What if I'm too old/too young, under qualified/over qualified, asking too much/too little?
- Am I making a fool of myself?
- Am I missing something – is there something else I should be doing?
- Will I mess up the interview?
- Did I say the right things – could I have done better?
- What if I get the job and it's not enough money or it's the other side of the country?
- What if there are no jobs that I can do?

Self-image
- Is it my fault? Could I have prevented it? What if it happens again?
- Do I have a say in things now that I have no job?
- What will people think, do they think I deserved it – that I'm a layabout?
- How do I introduce myself now and what do I say when people ask me what I do?
- Will I end up on the street; is this the start of the slippery slope?

Relationships
- Have I lost my partner's/children's respect?
- Will I lose my friends?
- How can I keep up with my social life when I'm worried about money?
- Is my family angry with me and do they disapprove of me?
- Does my partner resent the burden I've put on them?
- How can I give the children what they need?
- Who would want to go out with someone unemployed?

OVERCOMING WORRY: WHAT TO DO ABOUT IT

Accept that there are areas for *concern* when unemployment occurs. Changes to need to be made, finances do have to be sorted out, the future does need to be reassessed. It is also a sad fact of life that friendships may change and relationships suffer.

A degree of worry is perfectly natural. It signals that there are problems to deal with. Someone who seems totally unworried, or professes complete unconcern, might not be coping with things as well as they appear to be.

If, however, your thoughts seem to be intrusive or compulsive in a way that you find difficult to cope with, then go and see your doctor and explain the situation to them.

The best way of coping with worry is to look consciously at the problems and aim to arrive at the best constructive solution available in all the circumstances.

Make time for problems

Worry happens when we know there are problems that we haven't resolved. By setting aside specific times to look at them, less time need be spent worrying about them.

Set up special 'worry time' to think about solving problems:

- Learn to recognize when you are worried. What do you tend to worry about? What sort of thoughts do you have?
- Set aside twenty to thirty minutes every day – at the same time each day if possible – and call this 'worry time'. Use this time to think about problems and try out problem-solving methods to eliminate them. See *Problem Solving* on p.76.
- Now that you have a definite time to concentrate on worrying every day, it's perfectly all right to forget to worry at other times.

WORRY

- When you worry outside this time, tell yourself firmly to postpone it until your proper 'worry time'. Write down the worry if you are worried you might forget it in the meantime.
- Make full use of your 'worry time'. Don't let other concerns push it to one side.

If, despite being firm, worries still intrude outside the time set aside for them, try one or more of the following:

- Do something pleasant to take your mind off it.
    - Get moving. It's difficult to be physically active and worry at the same time. Exercise, take part in a sport or team game, play with the children, walk the dog.
- Lose yourself in another world. Read a gripping novel, look out for your favourite programmes on television, watch a film, hire a video.
    - Use your hands. Simple, practical things can be very soothing. Sort something out, repair something, knit, sew, crochet, do some planting, weed the garden, knead dough to make bread.
    - Make a list of things at a time when you feel good so that you can have it to hand when worry sets in.
- Practise a 'thought stopping' technique:
    - Picture a big red STOP sign.
    - Practise saying the word STOP to yourself firmly and with authority.
    - When your thoughts seem to be turning into nagging worries, say the word STOP to yourself and picture the red STOP again.
- Tell yourself that you will deal with this at the appropriate time then get on with something else.
- Practice will make this technique almost automatic.
- Use positive affirmations to change your thoughts:
    - Affirmations are positive thoughts that replace the worrying ones.
    - Pick a positive statement that counteracts the feeling of worry

Examples
'I am relaxed and capable'
'I am making the choices I wish to make'
'I have all that I need to do the best that I can'
'The world is a good and positive place'
'I am calm and strong'

- When you find worrying thoughts going round and round your brain, repeat the affirmation instead.
- Practise the relaxation exercises set out in the chapter on *stress* (see p.67). This will help prevent worry from turning into stress.

PROBLEM SOLVING

There are methods of problem solving that you could use to make your 'worry time' more constructive.

Mostly, when we worry, we ask ourselves questions that we don't know the answer to, or to which we have no answers. One technique for problem solving is to ask ourselves a series of constructive questions.

What am I worried about?
Identify your worries and clarify what you are worried about. Write down what it is.

Example
'I'm worried that I won't be able to afford Christmas presents this year.'

What can I do about it?
Think about the possible solutions to the problem. Write them down without criticizing or judging them. Aim to try for at least five solutions, more if possible.

Example
- I could make things instead of buying them.
- I could promise to do a service for people instead of giving an object.

- I could sell something to get money.
- I could do short-term seasonal work to get money.
- I could tell them I'm not celebrating Christmas this year.
- I could throw a party for everyone instead.
- I could club together with someone else.
- I could buy on credit and hope things get better in the new year.
- I could explain how things are and just give token gifts.
- I could quarrel with everyone just before Christmas and not buy anything.

What do I want to happen?
All the solutions fit the bare outline of the problem, but some are more attractive than others. Think about all the things you want any solution to achieve.

Example
- I want everyone to enjoy Christmas
- I want to have a good Christmas without feeling I'm scrimping.
- I want people to think well of me – for my own self-respect.

What do I decide?
Choose those solutions that offer the best fit. One solution may be perfect, or you may combine two or three.

Example
- I am an excellent woodworker so I'll make a couple of the presents for people that I know like that sort of thing.
- I'll sell my mountain bike to get some extra cash for the other presents.
- I'll use some of that money to give a party for friends.
- I'll give Jane and Tom babysitting vouchers – I promise to babysit for free any time they need me.

What do I need to do to put it into practice?
What are the steps that result from the solutions that you have chosen?

Example
- Put ad in local paper to sell bike.
- Design attractive babysitting vouchers to make a nicer present.
- Design and cost woodwork projects.
- Plan and cost a party.

Once you have chosen a solution, keep to it and act on it. Accept that you will have doubts as it is never possible to know the exact outcome.

Having defined the problem and considered a number of solutions you have done everything you can to arrive at the best decision.

7
ANGER

WHAT IS ANGER?
The word 'anger' can cover a number of very negative emotions – rage, jealousy, frustration, hate or resentment. What they all have in common is the gut-wrenching, stomach-churning, fist-clenching physical feelings they produce.

When we think of anger we often think of the outward signs of rage such as shouting, stamping, and so on – but anger can turn inwards too. When it does this it produces a quieter but equally destructive sense of bitterness and self-loathing.

In the right place, at the right time, anger is a useful emotion to have. It acts as an alarm bell alerting us to injustice, unfairness, frustration, wrongdoing and threats to our well-being.

When feelings of anger are appropriate we can act constructively and productively in a situation, if we can stay in control and behave rationally. These feelings can help us to look after ourselves, achieve our goals and protect our rightful interests.

However, when anger becomes ingrained, inappropriate, or out of control, then it can tempt us to behave irrationally, hurtfully, destructively, even against our own interests. We react unsuitably and unproductively in a way which often just fuels our rage and resentment, making the situation even more difficult.

Sometimes, we find ourselves in circumstances where feelings of anger let us know that there is a problem, although there is nothing that we can do about it. In such a situation we can lose control of our anger. The entirely appropriate anger that we originally felt about a specific event gets lost in a rising ride of rage and frustration.

This is when anger becomes destructive and dangerous. It can happen quickly, boiling over in a matter of moments, or it can happen over a period of months or even years.

Symptoms of anger

irritation	brooding	fault-finding
aggression	physical tension	picking arguments
short temper	self-destructive behaviour	loss of humour
hostility	feeling threatened	

WHY MIGHT YOU FEEL ANGER?

Redundancy and unemployment are events that naturally give rise to much anger and frustration.

Anger can express itself in a number of different ways, and can be aroused by many different things. Many of those things that provoke anger are present in redundancy and unemployment:

Defensive anger
Aroused by criticism, disapproval and rejection.

Redundancy can feel very much like rejection. We also fear disapproval and criticism from friends and family for losing our job and, perhaps, for failing to find another quickly. Applications for jobs, with these sorts of feelings, may feel like an open invitation to yet more criticism and rejection.

Fearful anger
Aroused by threat to well-being.

Being unemployed can feel very threatening to our well-being. We feel uncertain about our future security and can feel great anger at those who seem to be responsible for it, or threaten it in any way.

Hurt anger
Aroused by lack of appreciation, unfairness, betrayal, neglect.

Being made redundant after years of hard work can feel extremely unfair. It can also feel like a betrayal by our employer. Unanswered or unsuccessful job applications can also feel like neglect and lack of appreciation.

Jealousy
Aroused by exclusion.

Unemployment can lead to feelings of jealousy against those who have what we feel should be ours, too. It can be hard to see others being 'included' in paid employment when we feel rejected by it. Former colleagues may be seen as competitors for limited resources rather than as allies.

Frustration
Aroused by obstructions.

Redundancy usually means having to replan and rethink our aims and ambitions. Even with realistic, well-thought-out goals it can be hard to get back on track and every setback can feel like a major obstacle.

OVERCOMING ANGER: WHAT TO DO ABOUT IT

It is important to recognize and accept that you are angry about what has happened.

Anger is justified – nobody wants to sit back and passively accept unemployment without making their feelings known. But it is also important to channel that anger into productive channels instead of letting it fester.

We need to find safe ways of releasing excess pent-up anger

so that we can work constructively towards our own interests.

To channel the anger of unemployment in particular, follow as much of the advice as possible in *Part One: Things that help*. For example:

- Take steps to build up your self-confidence and self-worth. When these are low, anger often becomes unproductive.
- Set realistic goals for yourself. Don't let anger and frustration rob you of your aims and ambitions.
- Maintain as many of the structures and benefits as possible that you formerly achieved through paid work. Your well-being will feel less threatened.
- Maintain your contacts and social links. Don't let jealousy and hostility isolate you.
- Think positively and channel your energy productively, you will feel less defensive and hurt.
- Be nice to yourself.
- Get some support.
- Update your skills and develop your education. Success is a great antidote to anger.

If, however, anger itself is preventing you from doing this, the following self-help methods may be useful.

Physical release
The physical release of the tension associated with anger, frustration and aggression can be very beneficial. Bottling up emotions is harmful, but so is expressing them destructively. Safe physical releases include:
- Hard physical labour – digging the garden, scrubbing floors, chopping wood.
- Competitive sport – team games can provide a regular outlet.
- Strenuous exercise – running, swimming, aerobics, anything vigorous.

- Shouting – choose somewhere harmless, or shout into a pillow.
- Pillow punching – can be combined with shouting.

Emotional release

Anger creates emotional tension as well as physical tension.

We feel resentment and frustration and want to say things that are much better left unsaid. As with physical tension, bottling it all up can be harmful. But just letting go and getting everything off your chest can be damaging to relationships and harm your self-respect.

You can get emotional release from anger by trying one or more of the following methods:

- **Writing letters –** write down all your grievances to whoever you wish, fully and comprehensively, but remember to *destroy them* afterwards.

- **Anger list –** write a list of all that you are angry about – *'I am angry with . . . because . . .'*

    ### Example
    - I am angry with Helen because she didn't invite me to the party.
    - I am angry with the children for moaning about money.
    - I am angry with Mr White because he ignored my request for help.

When you have written down all the reasons for your anger, look back over your list and ask yourself what you would have *preferred* to happen in each case.

Example
- I would have preferred Helen to ask me to the party.

- I would have preferred the children to understand and be reasonable.
- I would have preferred Mr White to have listened to me and helped.

Doing this helps you to start to think more calmly about things that have made you angry.

- **Rights list** – write a list of the things that you feel that nobody has the right to do to you – *'Nobody has the right to . . .'*

    Example
    - Nobody has the right to treat me as second rate.
    - Nobody has the right to tell me what to do.
    - Nobody has the right to ignore me.

After writing down all you can, look back over your list and write down all the things that this means you *do* have a right to – *'I have a right to . . .'*

    Example
    - I have a right to be treated well.
    - I have a right to my independence.
    - I have a right to be taken seriously.

Doing this helps you to see more clearly the roots of some of your resentment and frustration, and you can begin to think more clearly about it.

- **Talking it through** – choose someone you trust to listen to you without interrupting or telling you what to do. Ask them first if they are willing to help you by listening to you, but don't be hurt if they say they can't – find someone else instead.

- **Laughter** – take all the opportunities you can to laugh. Search out as many as possible – watch all the comedy programmes on television, spend time with people who can let go and be silly, play with children, read books and magazines you find funny. Laughter can release both the physical and the emotional tension of anger and restore a sense of perspective.

8
APATHY

WHAT IS APATHY?
Sometimes, we can become so overwhelmed with stress, worry or anger, that the emotions become too much and we stop feeling or doing anything at all. Everything comes to a full stop. Nothing bothers us much and nothing seems very important any more. Life seems dull, empty and meaningless, but at least it doesn't hurt so much.

Apathy can creep up gradually without us noticing it, or it can happen overnight – a bit like the old joke: 'my get-up-and-go just got up and went'.

Everything becomes too much effort and there seems to be no reward in doing anything. Why bother to go out, for example. It's such an effort to get dressed, get there and anyway you won't enjoy it.

Gradually, we come to do less and less and slip deeper and deeper into apathy. Because we attempt less, life becomes unexciting and holds fewer and fewer rewards. The world becomes unstimulating and ceases to hold our interest.

Apathy can also be a self-fulfilling prophecy. Especially so if we are feeling let down about losing our job or failing an interview. There may, quite unconsciously, be an argument that runs through our head saying, 'I must be no good; I'll show I'm no good; I'll do nothing and get nowhere and *prove* I'm no good'.

Symptoms of apathy

everything seems too much trouble	avoiding effort
boredom	pessimism
lack of interest	suspicion of anything new
sense of meaninglessness	passivity

avoiding people
putting off tasks
negative thinking
resigned to life

low self-worth
hopelessness
repetition of unsatisfying routines

WHY MIGHT YOU EXPERIENCE APATHY?

Getting back into work can seem like an overwhelming and impossible task.

We start out with high hopes, but one or two setbacks – a bad interview, no replies to applications, a few days or weeks with nothing suitable to apply for – and our first enthusiasm begins to wane. We begin to slow down and be more cautious.

In some ways, this is no bad thing.

You are more likely to achieve success with a realistic picture of the situation, than with blind optimism. But when disillusionment begins to slide into despair you may stop planning realistic, practical strategies, and become apathetic instead.

Apathy prevents us from doing anything constructive, whilst giving the illusion of shielding us from a number of unpleasant things:

- **Disappointment** – if we take no risks then we aren't open to the very unpleasant feelings of frustration and defeat that happen when the risk doesn't come off.

    We willingly forfeit the thrill of achievement in return for not feeling the pain of disappointment.

- **Failure** – if we fail, we have to cope with what can feel like a severe blow to our self-esteem. When this happens, apathy can protect a frail ego.

> If we never attempt anything, we will never fail and never have to feel foolish. Neither will we have to defend ourselves against criticism, or try to excuse or explain ourselves.

- **Success** – if we take a risk and succeed, there are other problems to face. If we are successful and get that job, can we will cope with the responsibility after all this time?

    Life may change for the better, but it's still going to change, and *any* change causes stress.

- **Uncertainty** – the situation we find ourselves in may not be very good or very pleasant but at least we know that we can deal with it – just about!

    If we take risks, do things, try to make changes, who knows where we might end up, or how we will cope.

When difficult emotions are already overwhelming us, the last thing we want to do is to risk adding to them. We avoid doing anything that may upset the precarious balance that we have achieved.

In the long term, of course, taking action could actually solve the problem but it's hard to see it this way when you're so caught up in it.

Unfortunately, the longer apathy continues, the harder it is to break out of it.

Feelings of apathy may diminish, but because things have been left to slide, our problems look worse and can actually be even more difficult to solve.

It's tempting to think that the easiest way to deal with them is to drift back into apathy again and pretend that it doesn't matter. Unfortunately the result is simply a slow downward spiral that takes an enormous amount of energy to break out of.

OVERCOMING APATHY: WHAT TO DO ABOUT IT

To combat apathy, you need to keep doing constructive things to build your future. Even the smallest actions will keep alive a sense of progress.

When the feelings of apathy eventually diminish, it's not too hard to pick up the threads and get back on course.

Keep moving forward

Some of the advice in *Part One: Things that help* is especially good for combating apathy. Of special relevance are:

- *Maintain as many as possible of the structures and benefits that you formerly achieved through paid work.*

By keeping a meaningful routine in your life, you know where you are and what you should be doing. You don't have to keep making decisions about what to do or where to go next – apathy makes this difficult. You will also minimize the amount of change that you have to deal with.

- *Take steps to build up your self-confidence and self-worth.*

It is very hard to continue to feel apathetic when you feel confident and good about yourself.

- *Maintain your contacts and social links.*

This can be difficult to do in the face of apathy, but if you make the effort, it is amazing how other people's energy can rub off on you. They can take you out of yourself, and help to motivate you. It also means that you haven't cut yourself off from your sources of support.

Other things such as updating and developing your skills and education, setting goals and thinking positively are useful ways of staving off apathy and preventing it from setting in.

Keeping going

Specific ways of making sure that you still continue to move forward, even when apathy strikes, include the following methods:

- *Find a friend or a group to do things with.*

Company can help lighten the most tedious load and provide moral support at the lowest times. It's also helpful and builds self-esteem to find yourself giving support to others in their turn.

- *Make sure you give yourself small, regular, rewards.*

Concentrating on the big rewards, like getting a job, can seem too difficult and far away to have any real meaning. Give yourself more immediate treats as well after completing each stage of a task – after writing a letter or making a phone call, for example.

- *Remind yourself what the rewards are.*

The big rewards may seem a long way off and difficult to keep in mind, so make a list of all the things you hope to gain by keeping going. Keep the list and look at it regularly to remind yourself what you are heading towards.

- *Make sure you continue to do things you enjoy.*

Even if you don't actually feel you are enjoying them, it is important to remind yourself that there *are* things that you enjoy. Pleasure needs the opportunity to break through.

- *Break things down into manageable chunks.*

Do a little bit at a time – at least you will feel that you are doing something. The little bits will add up to more than you imagine. Aim to finish each chunk, and reward yourself accordingly, rather than worrying about completing the whole thing.

- *Avoid putting things off.*

Don't wait for the perfect time. Don't wait until you're 'in the mood' – just do it.

- *Notice the things that you do achieve:*
  - Record every achievement, every success, no matter how small.
  - Think of one thing every day that you want to achieve. Congratulate yourself when you succeed.
  - Write a list of achievements to date – be very encouraging to yourself, don't set impossibly high standards.
  - Ask a friend to tell you what they think you have achieved in your life so far (choose someone who you can trust to speak well of you).

9
DEPRESSION

WHAT IS DEPRESSION?
If stress, worry and anger continue to overwhelm without being resolved in any way, then apathy may begin to deepen into depression.

Like apathy, depression is the body and mind's response to continued unpleasant emotions. We 'switch off' and become unable to respond to outside stimulus, even something pleasant or exciting.

Depression, however, goes much deeper than apathy, and can generate its own negative emotions of guilt, misery and anguish.

When you feel depressed, energy levels sink unusually low. Everything becomes an effort. Things that you once did automatically seem to be quite beyond you. It takes all your strength and will-power just to keep going.

As well as low energy, there are feelings of sadness or loss, the pain of guilt or shame, and often feelings of emptiness.

You may find yourself continually thinking back to a painful incident, reliving the unhappiness over and over again. You may reproach yourself for all sorts of things that have happened to you and your family, even though you know you are not really to blame.

Physical symptoms
Changed sleep patterns	frigidity or impotence
early waking	tiredness or exhaustion
changed appetite	lassitude
constant aches and pains	self-neglect

Emotional symptoms

- hopelessness
- pessimism
- lack of interest
- lack of pleasure
- poor memory
- frequent desire to cry
- loss of confidence
- inability to make decisions
- lack of concentration
- sense of guilt
- brooding
- emotional anguish
- low self-esteem

WHY MIGHT YOU FEEL DEPRESSED?

Losing your job can simply cause too many emotions for you to deal with at once; it's a very big shock. However gradual the build-up to job loss, however good the preparations, the actual event and aftermath are a severe blow.

In addition to shock, we also have to deal with loss. Depression and loss are closely linked. We all face loss and bereavement throughout our lives. The pain can last from a few hours – perhaps when a friend moves away – to many months or years when a close relative dies.

The loss we feel when we lose our job has several roots:

Loss of future

Until the moment when we find out we are to lose our job, we plan for the future that we assume will happen. Suddenly *that* particular future no longer exists. All the plans and hopes based on what we thought was going to happen have to be abandoned. Abandoning our hopes is painful, even when we can, eventually, replace them with others.

Loss of friends

Even if they are not close friends, the people that we work with are certainly familiar to us. We may have worked alongside them for many years, and gone through a lot together. Knowing that we may never see them again will be distressing.

Loss of identity
'*Who am I now I'm not a . . .?*' Often, we get used to thinking of ourselves solely in terms of our job. It becomes part of our identity. The question we get asked most, after our name, is what do we do for a living! It doesn't have to a high-status job for us to feel attached to what we do, even proud of it – and regret the loss of this aspect of our working lives.

Loss of function
When we lose our job, we may begin to wonder what purpose we serve, what our role in society is. Unless we have very strong interests outside work, much of our sense of usefulness and commitment is centred on the job we do. When we lose it, our sense of having a useful function may also be temporarily lost.

Loss of security
However kindly or professionally it's done, redundancy still feels like rejection. We no longer seem to belong to the places we used to, or with the people we used to belong with. There are no certainties any more; we feel insecure and uncertain. Being pushed out of the security of a group identity along with all our expectations, is painful.

Loss of stability
When we lose our job, we lose with it all the day-to-day routines that we may have built up over the years. We lose the regularity from our lives – regular hours, regular holidays, regular wage packets. We lose the order and stability that we have come to rely on.

OVERCOMING DEPRESSION: WHAT TO DO ABOUT IT
If at *any* time you suspect that the depression you feel is getting too much for you to handle on your own, go and see your doctor immediately. Doctors are used to treating depression and have the experience, training and resources

to help you. Don't suffer unnecessarily.

When you feel depressed, it is important to act early to prevent the onset of a deeper depression. Although it's important to find constructive solutions to your problems, this is not the best time to deal with them. Instead, give yourself time away from your concerns and be kind to yourself. This is easier said than done when you are feeling low, but when practised persistently, the rewards are very real.

Put problems in their place
Practise setting aside a special time each day for looking at problems. The way to do this is outlined in the chapter dealing with *worry* (see p.74). There is also a useful problem-solving technique in the same chapter. The reason for doing this is to reassure yourself that you are not letting things slide. Putting problems to one side temporarily, allows you to concentrate on looking after yourself and feeling better.

Keep up with the things that are most important – these may include: paying bills; keeping in contact with friends; maintaining family ties. Do just what you feel able to do. Leave everything else for your problem-solving time or until you feel better.

Be nice to yourself
Practise being very good to yourself for the rest of the time.

First of all, accept that what has happened to you has been a great shock and, although it may have been months ago, you are reacting in an entirely appropriate way. Shock sometimes takes time to work its way through to the surface.

Accept that you have been under stress, and that now you need a break from problems. Aim to be kind to yourself so that you can recover and carry on with the rest of your life.

Accept, also, that there is no need for you to cling to this pain as some sort of punishment for what has happened.

Be kind to your body
Some of the things that you could treat yourself to might include:

Rest and sleep
Depression has happened because of an overload of stress and negative emotions and it is important that you rest and recuperate if you are to feel better.

Rather than just slip into lethargy, make definite times to relax and rest during the day. You could practise the physical and mental relaxation techniques outlined in the section *Getting relaxed* (see p.67). Alternatively, you could just listen to some relaxing music.

Because depression can alter your sleep patterns, you may need to give extra attention to sleeping well. Make sure that:

- You are warm enough. Being depressed can lower your body temperature slightly, leaving you constantly chilly.
- You only use your bedroom for relaxing and pleasant things. Find another room for writing job applications, paying bills, etc.
- Your bedroom is pleasant – warm and softly lit. Replace any harsh, 100 watt bulbs with 40 or 60 watt bulbs – try pink or apricot tints.
- Relax before getting into bed. A warm bath or a soothing drink – milk or chocolate, not alcohol – can be good, so can winding down by listening to music.
- If you are prone to waking during the night, make sure that something comforting to eat and drink are at hand. An undemanding book or the radio can be useful too.

- If you are very restless, get up and do something – don't lie awake worrying. Put lights and heating on, though – don't sit alone in the cold and the dark.

Physical exercise

Even thinking about exercise can be difficult when you are feeling down and tired. But it is important to take some physical exercise in order to disperse underlying tensions, and to promote a healthy tiredness instead of an unhealthy exhaustion.

For these purposes, the exercise needn't be elaborate. A short walk in the fresh air to the shops or around the park every day will do more good than a high-powered aerobics class once a week. Take the dog, or offer to walk someone else's, if an enthusiastic walking companion would help to get you moving.

Cycling and swimming are also good exercises for giving a sense of exhilaration and movement.

Touch

It's not just emotional feelings that can become suppressed during depression – physical feelings and sensations can become flattened as well.

Touch is soothing and healing. Animals and children who have been orphaned young and haven't touched or hugged enough, become very depressed and fail to thrive.

It is helpful to keep your sense of touch alive:

- If you have pets, take extra time in the day to stroke and groom them.
- Get regular massage. It needn't be expensive, professional treatment.
- Look after your own body. Keep fit, exercise or work out.

Water
Water seems to give us great comfort. Being in, or on, water can be relaxing or invigorating depending on what we are doing. Try:

- Showers – for invigoration and letting the water wash away your worries.
- Deep baths – add music, scented bath oils and warm towels for extra relaxation.
- Swimming – relaxing or strenuous, depending on how you feel.

Comfort food
Now is the time that comfort eating comes into its own. Within the framework of a healthy diet, eating favourite foods can provide great satisfaction. Think back to your childhood; what did you enjoy then? What do you enjoy when you're recovering from a cold or flu? Most people seem to like sweet and creamy foods – sweetened cereals, creamy puddings, custard, chocolate, cake, ice-cream. Or they prefer 'childhood favourites' – bangers and mash, baked beans, tinned spaghetti, boiled egg with toast soldiers.

Plan your comfort eating as a treat for yourself, rather than as a basis for your normal diet – keep it as something special.

Be kind to your mind
Some of the things that you could treat yourself to might include:

Laughter
Treat yourself to laughter. You may not feel like it, but at least give yourself the maximum opportunity for laughter to break in on a regular basis:

- Search out comedy programmes on television and radio.

- Borrow 'comedy classic' tapes from the library.
- Choose to rent humorous videos rather than serious ones.
- Read books and magazines you find funny.
- See people who you know you can have a laugh with.
- Do things that you remember used to be fun and make you laugh.

Music
Music has enormous power to change moods. Listening to relaxing music has already been mentioned, but try listening to upbeat music, as well, during the day. Even if it's not the sort of thing you would usually listen to, try a different radio station or visit the local library for light classics and cheerful, popular pieces to lift your spirits.

Escape
Lose yourself in a book. Absorbing books such as thrillers, romances, and mysteries make good escapist reading, as do whodunits. If your concentration is low, try rereading old favourites. Often, favourite childhood books and children's classics are perfect escape material – absorbing and undemanding.

You can lose yourself in films, videos, and TV programmes as well. Make sure they have a good, easy-to-follow plot and a gripping storyline. Oddly enough, 'weepies' can sometimes be quite beneficial. Becoming involved with the problems of fictional characters can take your mind off your own and can also provide a release for tears that are proving hard to shed.

Quietness
You've had a tough time. Along with rest and sleep for your body (see above) treat yourself to peace and quietness of mind:

- Take time to be quiet and alone with yourself on a reg-

ular basis. You sometimes need to get away from other people's demands and expectations, however kindly meant.
- Meditate. It's not difficult and it's very peaceful:
  - Give yourself ten minutes or so.
  - Sit in a quiet, comfortable place where you are unlikely to be disturbed. Make sure that your clothing is comfortable and that you will be warm enough.
  - Close your eyes.
  - Breathe in and out gently through your nose. Concentrate on each breath as you breathe, feeling the air as it moves in and out.
  - Imaging each out-breath carrying away all the pain and stress and tension from your body.
  - Imagine each in-breath bringing in freshness and lightness and peace.
  - If you wish, you can repeat a calming word to yourself, such as 'peace', 'still' or 'calm', as you breathe.
  - If your thoughts drift, gently bring them back to concentrating on your breathing. If other thoughts come into your mind, don't worry – just acknowledge them and let them go; you can deal with them when you have finished.
  - At the end of the time you have allowed yourself, open your eyes, stretch, and get up slowly and gently.
- Go to peaceful places:
  - Get out into the country.
  - Old buildings – churches, museums – are often tranquil.
  - Parks are quiet during school hours.
  - Being by water is very peaceful – walk by a river or sit by a lake.
  - The sea can be calming or exhilarating, depending on it's own mood.
  - Plants are soothing to be with – they don't argue or make judgements.

Dealing with guilt

Uncomfortable feelings of guilt or shame often accompany depression.

One way of coping with guilt is very similar to that suggested for coping with worry – set aside a special regular time for looking at the things you feel guilty about:

- Learn to recognize when you are feeling guilty or remorseful. Do your thoughts keep straying back to previous painful events? Do you constantly condemn yourself for past mistakes?
- Set aside twenty to thirty minutes a day, every day, until you decide the guilty feelings are dealt with. Use this time to confront and accept past incidents:

  1. Identify, and write down, what it is that you feel guilty about.

Example
I feel guilty about letting Andrew down over the car boot sale.

  2. Write down whatever it is that you said or did that caused it to happen.

Example
I was too lazy to find out about it, then it seemed like an enormous problem, and in the end I left it too late to book a space.

  3. Look at what you have written, and decide what the *facts* are. If there are any points that are not factually true, then cross them out.

Example
~~I was too lazy to find out about it, then it seemed like an enormous problem, and in the end~~ I left it too late to book a space.

4. Looking at what happened, decide if there is anything that you can do, or anything that you would like to do, to make amends. (There doesn't *have* to be anything.)

Example
I could arrange it for another weekend and make all the arrangements myself so that I don't need to bother Andrew with it.

5. Looking at what happened, is there anything that you would do differently in the future?

Example
Next time, I'll do things before they assume overwhelming proportions. I'll make sure I reward myself when I do things at once until it gets to be a habit.

- Once you have gone through this process and confronted the incident that is causing you to feel guilty, ask yourself how much of it was actually your fault.

While not seeking to blame others for what happened, perhaps things could have been clarified or handled differently. This might help you to avoid the same problem in the future.

- When your time is up for that day, firmly put your guilt to one side.

If you find your thoughts straying back to it during the day, practise some of the ideas for stopping worrying. You can find these set out in the chapter on *worry* (see p.74).

CONCLUSION: TEN POSITIVE STEPS

The bad news is that most of us can expect to be made redundant once in our careers. That's just the way the world of work is now – companies come and go at a much faster rate than they ever did in the past.

The good news though, is that redundancy no longer carries the stigma it once used to, and there is more help available than ever before. Rather than dreading redundancy, use it as an opportunity to take stock and build a better future.

If I had to condense the advice in this book into ten essential steps that ensured you not only survived redundancy but prospered too, they would be:

Step 1. Check your finances

- Make an appointment to see an Advisor with the Employment Service immediately. They will work out what benefits you are entitled to and ensure that you get National Insurance credits.
- Take time to find out exactly how much money you have, and how much you spend each month. Work out a budget that will keep you going over the long term.
- Get financial advice. You may have a substantial redundancy payment to invest, so get the best help you can – consult at least three sources before committing yourself to anything.

Step 2. Stand back and look at your life

Re-assess what you're doing, and where you're going. Plan what happens next. Are you doing what you really want to?

If not, this could be the chance to change direction.

- List your skills and achievements. What has given you the biggest thrill, and what are you proudest of?
- Find out more about the career you've always fancied – the Careers Service or your library are good places to start.
- Think about *how* you want to work – there are many more choices these days. Perhaps being self-employed, freelance, or working part-time would suit you better.

Step 3. List all the things you enjoyed about working

- Keep them in mind when looking for another job.
- Rather than miss out, find ways to get enjoyment from the other things in your life.

Step 4. List all the things you'll be glad to see the back of

- Celebrate never having to do them again.
- Analyze what's at the root of your dislike, and use this to think about what you want in the future.

Step 5. Set yourself goals

- Work out what you want to achieve and set yourself the daily, weekly, and monthly targets that will get you there.
- Celebrate when you attain each of your targets, and remind yourself how far you've come.

Step 6. Build up your confidence.

- Find ways to continue to do the things you enjoy and are good at.
- Be good to yourself – treat yourself well both

physically and mentally.
- Take your aims and ideals seriously, and get working on them.

Step 7. Take job hunting seriously

These days it's a professional business – get up to date with the latest skills and techniques.

- Join your local Jobclub. They can give you professional help and advice, as well as free stationery, postage, phone calls, periodicals and journals, etc. It's available through your Employment Centre after six months' registered unemployment.
- Do your research. Find out about suitable companies and approach them directly by letter or by phone. Don't just rely on advertised vacancies.
- Use your network. Ask for *advice* and *information* from friends, colleagues, former contacts, customers, suppliers, fellow professionals, everyone.

Step 8. Plan to go back into work fitter and better qualified than you left

Now you have the time, spend some of it on yourself. Think about improving your:

- Physical health – Think about diet and exercise.
- Stress levels – Take time to rest and relax.
- Qualifications – Find out what's available in your area. Many adult education courses are offered at reduced rates for benefit recipients. You may also be eligible for free training through the Employment Service Training For Work programme. (This is not just for plumbing and brick-laying, whatever you might have heard. Some of these courses are the equivalent of HNC/HND level.)

Step 9. Unburden yourself
It's pointless trying to pretend that nothing has happened.

- Talk things through with family and friends and get their support.
- Spread the emotional load among those who are willing to help you – don't expect one person to take it all.
- Do things that take you out of yourself as well, though – you deserve a respite.

Step 10. Decide to survive
This is a turning point in your life. Become one of the people who pick themselves up, dust themselves down, and get on with life:

- Put the bitterness and hurt firmly behind you and focus on the future.
- Keep going – do something towards at least one of your goals every day.